The Man You're Meant to Be

John Simons

The Man You're Meant to Be

A Call of Self-Examination for Every Believer, Hypocrite, and Outsider

B&H
PUBLISHING®
BRENTWOOD, TENNESSEE

Printed in the United States of America

979-8-3845-2201-0

Published by B&H Publishing Group
Brentwood, Tennessee

Dewey Decimal Classification: 155.3
Subject Heading: MASCULINITY /
MEN / CHRISTIAN LIFE

Cover design and illustration by Matt Stevens.

1 2 3 4 5 6 • 28 27 26 25

For my son, Noah.

Contents

Despair settles within our bones
Our precious time rusts away
All that I cherish deteriorates
Everything I have left to hold
Will come to a close

We labor endlessly
Only to raise tattered hands
We could rupture every levee
And still, it would never be enough

For every one we mend
We sever a hundred
For every good we build
We tear down another thousand

We lift our praise
To cover each other's eyes
How deceiving we can be
When we neglect the accruing cost

But for you, my son
I will not turn your gaze
Ignorance will not pave your way

When I leave you
I will walk into dusk
Learn from these fractured steps
Listen carefully and heed these words I speak
A Wisdom that was not of me

Introduction

This book is about growing into the man God called us to be. It's about the narrow path every man is called to journey upon, as we are formed into the image of Jesus. Too often, our conceptions of manhood do not centrally revolve around the formation, teachings, and work of Christ himself. And any view of manhood that does not begin and end with Jesus's life is no biblical view at all. He illuminates our true calling and identity as image bearers of God—drawing us closer to our good heavenly Father, inviting us to surrender to a Spirit-led life, as we learn to cultivate wisdom from *above*.

At the heart of this book is an invitation to walk *with* God. That's not to be dismissive of the fact that each year we grow more and more biblically illiterate as a culture and nation. It's a major problem. However, we won't solve our crisis of manhood by merely learning more *about* God. Rather, we must get to know him by learning his ways. The journey of becoming a godly man begins by surrendering ourselves to him—the good, bad, and ugly. Our cultivation of true wisdom must be empowered by the Spirit, helping us arrive at vulnerable self-examination before his throne. We need to be convicted that we need less of ourselves, less of our ways, and more of Christ and his way if we are to become a man like him.

You'll recognize there are two parts of this work—the central task of part 1 is to help each man grasp what kind of wisdom is currently taking root and influencing our deepest desires and pursuits (because there isn't just one). Part 2 meets us in the trenches of life. The goal of the book is to help each of us foster a deeper relationship with God, cultivate godly character and wisdom, and become the presence we need to be for our wife, kids, family, and friends. It's to meet the call to walk on the narrow path of discipleship. However, as we venture on this path, we also must reconcile our assumptions about God, what we project onto our relationship with him, and meet him for who he really is.

Yet, to be clear, this book isn't just for men inside the walls of the church who wish to grow deeper in their faith. It's also for those who no longer walk through its doors, whether because they've been wounded by its people or become disenfranchised by what occurs inside its walls. If we're honest about the conversation between men and the church, those inside and outside are angry, cynical, discouraged, and frustrated. And more than likely, they feel like outsiders in a world that doesn't seek to equip or affirm them in leading, caring for, and serving like a godly man should.

However, the world doesn't get to dictate the narrative of how things ought to be—God and his Word are the final authority. So, even in a twisted, wayward world, we must remain steadfast, meeting our true call to grow into Christlikeness as we lead, love, and care for our families, friends, and community in the trenches of life. Above all else, our deepest desires should revolve around pursuing those ends for the glory of God.

I've prayed that this book falls in the hands of the addicted, defeated, empty, and lonely. We aren't meant to walk through life alone, and I hope this book encourages each of you to step forward in courage to seek after such. I promise it'll be worth it. And I would be remiss not to point out that this work is especially for those who currently hold shame around their necks, like a noose that suffocates the true joys of life. Each of us has blind spots and wounds that need mending. I hope this is just a first step in many men's lives to hand over their burdens to our good Shephard.

As we set out on the journey together, may we also each find another brother who's walking on the same narrow path of discipleship. In a world that's largely void of intentionality, friendship, and mutual spurring on, this book can be an opportunity to find each of those. May we each experience the depths of God's love and grace and recognize, as men, that we are to lead with the same posture of care and wisdom of our good Father.

Part 1

Navigating the Cultural Landscape

1

True Wisdom in a Wayward World

"Our heart is restless until it rests in you."[1]
St. Augustine

For all the modern technology in our world, times haven't changed as much as we think. Certainly, our basic quality of life in the twenty-first century has drastically improved, even since the early 1900s. Yet, with every giant step forward in innovation, we seem to only be reminded that behind every machine is still a human. A sophisticated, complex, yet flawed person, who longs for beauty, meaning, and happiness. Though the truth is, we still battle the same demons and wayward desires as those who stood in his place a thousand years ago. As true wisdom continues to remind us, there is nothing new under the sun, or afoot in human history (Eccles. 1:9).

No matter the historical period—we find stories of good men who set out to do hard things. We find heroes of war, artists and intellectuals who crafted their work into masterpieces, and true leaders among the ordinary who pushed forward in conviction when others would not. We find loving and courageous fathers, who did everything they could to ensure a better life for their families. We read of wild adventures of crossing oceans, trekking up mountains, breaking down on frontier plains, and enduring chilling ice storms because those brave enough wanted to be the first to do it. We discover men that sought God and found him.

But every coin has two sides, and so we also find tales of avoidable tragedy, heartache, sickness, and suffering. There's unchecked power that was left unconfronted and allowed to ransack the innocent. We encounter cowards and chameleons, who betrayed others for the sake of coin and influence. We uncover the reality that envy, greed, lust, and murder are found in every city. And we confront the fact that wickedness exists too, and it stalks and lures in those willing to walk in darkness. We see that real evil walks among us, and it lies behind the eyes of vile men, who seek to take the world and its people, as their own possession, through horrendous and disgusting acts.

Why do I say any of this? Because, if we study history long enough, eventually we stumble onto the great through line: everything and nothing have changed. The constant has always been the human condition, itself. And the men of this generation need to hear such and take heed and become the men God has called us to be in this world.

Just as it is with the history of humanity, the challenge and calling for us, as men, has not changed since the earliest of time. The same idols that sought to be worshipped on the altars of the first century are the ones that call for our attention, devotion, and sacrifice today. Yet, rather importantly, the same God who raised the dead, made the blind see, the deaf hear, gave rest to the weary, and freed the addicted calls us to build our lives on him. He calls us to be wise men who hear his words, practice them, and stand on his foundation (Matt. 7:24).

Throughout the rest of this work, we will be unpacking together what it means for our lives to reflect God's calling for us as men who represent him in this world. We will take heed on how to cultivate such a life. But the thing is: I don't think we should just assume we're already on that path; we must begin with discernment and self-examination before God on where we actually stand. That is the beginning of discovering true wisdom. I'll examine my own life, alongside yours. We're in this together.

I won't lie; this will require work. But if we truly desire to grow into the wise and godly men God calls us to be, we must recognize that this path is not for the faint of heart. This calling is a lifelong journey, full of setbacks and victories, mountaintops and valleys. And I'll acknowledge from the outset, becoming the men God intended us to be will never wholly happen until we meet Jesus face-to-face. So don't make this book a checklist. We can't outgrow or graduate from its lessons. We can only wrestle with its content in different ways during each of the changing seasons of life. In time these truths will also come alive and grow us in new ways. To grow into a wise and godly man is a call few take up, but no other journey is as rewarding to the soul.

Wells of Wisdom

It may sound strange, but the influence of wisdom in our lives is akin to a well we drink from each day. Every morning we lower our buckets down beneath the ground's surface, reel it back up, and take a heaping scoop to drink. Yet not everyone consumes the same quality of wisdom from their wells. Some of our wells are crystal clear, free of any impurities, while others are filled with something far murkier. Some of the wells we drink from have become so polluted with contaminants that it's difficult to ignore the reality that it's making its drinkers sick. However, the sad truth is that this man doesn't realize that he continues to drink what's killing him because he's never experienced fresh clean water. He's never been given a reason to question what is the difference between what's life-giving and toxic.

But now, stick with me. Imagine that our wisdom wells had more of a mystical nature. What if these wells did more than rehydrate our bodies but also replenished and influenced our will, values, and sense of meaning in life. What if their water guided our moral cravings and had the power to shape *who* we are, *what* we long for, seek to belong to, find satisfaction in, and yearn for approval/praise from. For every bucket of water we draw up, it not only has a bodily effect but a spiritual sway that either reinforces God's best for our lives or seeks to twist our deepest desires.

Here's the crux of the matter—this is how wisdom practically works in our lives. As Scripture reveals, the kind of wisdom we drink in ultimately guides our choices (even subconsciously). It conditions our thoughts and molds our character and habits to become *who* we are. It influences the deepest longings and desires of our heart and the ways we seek to find meaning. Wisdom is not just a bunch of old adages that help us find greater skill or understanding about life.

Don't miss this—wisdom is the formative source/power we draw upon to cultivate discernment and action in our lives. No matter the quality of the wisdom we are drawing up—we do so daily because we rely on it to navigate life's greatest tension points, everyday worries, seasons of chaos, disappointment, and success. There's a living component to the wisdom we drink in, as it shapes our decision-making to choose one of two different paths and destinations in life—and both are eternal in nature.

The right question then becomes, what kind of wisdom are we currently being guided by? Let me be clear because this is too important. Scripture doesn't suggest every kind of wisdom produces a better, more flourishing life. In fact, it warns us of the opposite condition—that we ought to be mightily aware of the possibility that we may be digesting and guided by a worldly wisdom, which eventually leads to our own downfall, devastation, and death—yet it will feel so satisfying going down.

Wisdom from Below

James, the half brother of Jesus, cautions us that there are two different kinds, or streams, of wisdom that can influence us. The first kind of wisdom he mentions is that from below, steeped in evil, sourced in the realm of the demonic. It stirs disorder, envy, fleshly desires, and every other vice one could imagine in those who are caught in its grip (James 3:14–16). The apostle Paul also speaks of this lower wisdom, as "the wisdom of this world" (1 Cor. 3:19). It's a false, or imitational, wisdom that promises us the world and the skill set to gain it. Though its followers might believe they're on a worthwhile journey toward success and influence, in reality, it's leading them down a set of crooked steps toward their eventual own self-destruction (Prov. 11:3).

In a fallen world, we each are tempted to drink it in because, initially, it tastes sweet, prompting the belief that it's enjoyable. But it's like a veiled poison, which gradually inflates our ego, producing an unquenchable thirst for success, acceptance, control, and influence in every sphere of our lives. At all costs.

Wisdom from below has a way of weaving itself into my thoughts in everyday ways. It called my name when I'm exhausted after a long week, and I selfishly believe that I'm owed sleeping in, or extra alone time (every introvert knows what I'm talking about). Or when I buy something over our typical budget and believe that I deserve this splurge because I'm the primary provider for our family. It uses the same line of reasoning to then suggest a late-night relapse of porn wouldn't hurt anyone but myself. Sometimes wisdom from below comes calling when I blatantly know I'm at fault in my marriage, and I consider the odds of whether I can successfully deflect ownership and place blame elsewhere.

It whispers in my ear, even now as I write this chapter. It tells me that if this book sells well enough, then I'll finally accept myself as valuable, worthy of love, and appreciation. I felt it seep into my soul when I was pastoring at one of the largest megachurches in history, and it told me to tie my identity to its status. And if I decided to walk away from it, no longer would anyone be impressed with me or value my voice as trustworthy. The phone calls from other growing churches asking for me to coach them on discipleship, small groups, or men's ministry would stop.

Wisdom from below was waiting to whisper to me outside the doors on my last day, slithering its voice into my mind that

I'd no longer matter or be important enough for those here to keep in touch with me. When I started having friendships with and earning the respect of other authors, pastors, and scholars, I heard its forked tongue say, "Don't you love that they respect you, John."

Notice a common theme for how wisdom from below attempts to work itself into our lives. It's a perverse invitation to make ourselves the absolute center of our world, to dominate, possess, and control the outcomes to our liking/acceptance/influence/version of joy.[2] It's listening to the snake in the garden of Eden and believing we too could become like God. We too can be knowledgeable and in control of all things and worthy of praise and glory (Gen. 3:5). Yet, at its core, it's evil, demonic, and worldly. Because that's exactly who's behind it—the devil, his demons, a wayward world, and your flesh—and they crave chaos, disorder, and rebellion in our lives (James 3:15).

I don't say any of this to scare you. It's merely a warning for both of us about the consequences of the wisdom we allow to shape us, as men. So let us not be ignorant—wisdom from below is a poison that slowly and shrewdly corrupts our mind, will, and desires. However, the irony is, the longer we drink in this poison, the greater the temptation grows to continue putting ourselves at the center of our world. And the greater our will is hollowed out from God's best for our life, the easier it becomes to be enslaved to the twisted passions and vices from below.

It's the ultimate plan of the devil to coerce us into following his false wisdom. Maybe this is already the wake-up call you needed in life—just as Christ calls you to surrender to him, so does the devil. The enemy desires for us to become like him, filled with twisted desires, and to carry out a life fulfilled in the crooked ways of the father of lies (John 8:44). He tempts us to believe we are gaining success or freedom to do as we please, but the opposite is true. The tragic part of being guided by wisdom from *below* is that all along we believe it was worth it, until the end, when we realize the terrifying weight of hitting rock bottom.

The truth is, we become what we love.[3] And ultimately, what we love shapes who we are and what/who we decide to worship in life. Wisdom from below pursues each of us, whispering in the shadows, tempting us to follow an empty inward descent that will send each of us hurling toward our own demise. I don't want this to be any man's life, and God doesn't want that to be your story. There is a different path we can take. There is a far better, richer, source of wisdom that we can drink in and allow to take root within our souls.

Wisdom from Above

Just as Paul modeled in the first century, we, too, can decide to walk in righteousness, putting our pride, ego, and sin to death and reject the ways of the world (Rom. 8:13; 1 Cor. 1:20). Maybe reading that sentence overwhelms you because you're stuck in shame. You loathe yourself for the sins you've committed or that you're still shackled to. If that's the case, I want to remind you that Paul was a former persecutor of Christians and felt every bit of the weight of sin you carry. Yet, God moved powerfully in and through him. No sin, past or present, can hold us back from God's calling in our life. As James describes, we can become a man filled with a wisdom not found in ourselves or this fallen world but from *above*: God himself (James 3:17–18).

I realize some of us reading right now are struggling to comprehend how the God of the universe, the maker of heaven and earth, would want anything to do with you. My friend, let go of the influence of the wisdom from *below*. Jesus does not carry himself in the ways we treat ourselves. The true wisdom he offers is sourced from his own love, goodness, and faithfulness. He did not come to earth to shun and turn us away but to offer rest from our weariness and relief from our heavy burdens (Matt. 11:28). Where each of us have condemned ourselves for self-destructive decisions and habits, he invites us to learn the depths of his gentleness and lowliness for you (Matt. 11:29–30).

Wisdom from above is tied to the heart of Christ. James characterizes it as pure, full of mercy, peace loving, sincere, and full of good fruit (James 3:17–18). To follow wisdom from above is to embrace a life defined by Christ's character and to be in an ever-deepening friendship with him as our risen Savior and King. It's to be Spirit-led in our formation, cultivating the character of a good godly man—being loving, joyful, peaceful, forbearant, kind, good, faithful, gentle, and self-controlled (Gal. 5:22–23). It's to have heard Jesus's words to the woman at the well, pondered them yourself, and chosen to desire a life shaped by eternity. It's to accept Jesus's offer to drink *living* water (John 4:10).

As we will discuss later, drinking in wisdom from *above* is neither a call to escape our world nor a need to feel like we must have life all put together and every sin under control. Rather, it's a life grounded in self-examination, repentance, confession, and trust in Christ's redeeming work on the cross. That is the starting place in learning the way of wisdom from above. It's a life surrendered to Jesus and to walk in fear and trembling before the Lord (Prov. 1:7). This book is an invitation to learn the great depths of his love and mercy for us, to live wisely, and to grow in Christlikeness. That's always been God's calling and challenge for each of us.

Wisdom and the Habit of Self-Examination Before God

Before the close of this chapter, I want to encourage each of us to find a quiet place and take as much time as we need to wrestle through these important, yet difficult, questions. Throughout the rest of the book, we will navigate through what God says about these very questions together.

Who am I yearning to become in this world?

Whom do I want to be fully known by?

Why is their love and acceptance so meaningful to me?

Who am I willing to lay down my life for?

How do I believe God sees me?

If you can write down the answers to these questions, then you've begun to do the hard work of self-examination. We have to peer below the surface and see what is influencing our deepest desires and longings. Maybe without ever realizing it to be the case. And you're not alone if you're anticipating not liking what you're going to find. Quite frankly, most of us don't. Yet, I hope each of us also comes to feel the immeasurable depths of God's grace in the following: The *fundamental* part is that we've begun to *recognize* and *acknowledge* what lies in the depths of our souls and the often-hidden destructive parts of our own self. And to recognize darkness in oneself is also to invite light to shine on it (John 1:5).

Now, think about your answers in relation to our discussion about the two sources, or kinds, of wisdom. Ask God to help bring clarity and a conversation around the following:

What kind of wisdom has shaped my answers?

Have I held back from honestly answering any question?

Where am I letting wisdom from below encroach into my life?

Do I trust God to be my foundation and source of wisdom in life?

Reflection and Group Discussion Questions

1. What did you learn about yourself by answering the closing questions of the chapter and later comparing them from the perspective of *wisdom from above* and *below*?

2. There's a temptation to think of *wisdom from above* and *below* in theoretical abstract terms. But how do you see each source of wisdom in our everyday life—in your personal life, at work, and in society?

3. Share a personal story of a time when you regret following the ways of *wisdom from below.*

4. If you found yourself identifying some of your *wisdom from below* (which we all are regularly tempted to do), what was the specific aspect of it? What are your plans, or whom can you invite in, to help you be accountable for this area of your life?

5. Where did you find hope and encouragement to greater grow in intimacy with God in this chapter? How has growing closer to God impacted your character and the way you live your life?

2

The Outsiders

"We make men without chests and expect of them virtue and enterprise. We laugh at honour and are shocked to find traitors in our midst. We castrate and bid the geldings be fruitful."[1]
C. S. Lewis

In Cormac McCarthy's novel *The Road*, a boy and his father navigate a postapocalyptic America as they head south to the Gulf Coast to avoid a deadly winter season.[2] Written primarily from the vantage point of the father, McCarthy portrays the calling and duty of manhood and fatherhood in such a beautiful, powerful, and yet sorrowful way. Not only must the father and son survive long days and nights maneuvering around the "bad guys" who are depraved cannibals, but they also must fight a more significant battle—holding onto their own humanity and moral integrity. A central facet of the story is the father teaching his son to "carry the fire." He must learn to walk in the ways of goodness and wisdom because, as we come to learn, the father is gravely sick. The father recognizes his son will soon face a future without his guiding presence and steady hand amid the chaos of a vile world.

The Road is a sobering tale, challenging us to consider the required sacrifices to become a good man. Even though none of us live in a dystopian environment, we have far more in common with this story than we might realize. Like the father with his son, we, too, face an ever-growing need to remember *who* we are and to hold onto our true humanity and purpose in a hell-bent world.

No, we aren't fending off cannibals or hordes of evil men driving around searching for their next victim. Instead, evil rears its head in other ways. On an individual level, the enemy desires to isolate us and ruin our lives by ushering us into a place of despair and withdrawal (1 Pet. 5:8). At the same time, on a more macro level, the enemy works to corrupt and dehumanize larger organizational structures, morals, and values of a given society so they reflect and worship him (John 12:31; 2 Cor. 4:4; Eph. 6:12). When we read the evils entrenched in the story of *The Road* and consider them as *absolute* evil, that's the devil's greatest scheme. He wants us to think he isn't afoot until we notice some gross malicious behavior. In reality, evil often comes by way of a subtle influence, eventually growing into a compounding force that can't easily be slowed in culture—just think of how Hitler's influence grew prior to World War II.[3]

The ways of the Enemy and his minions are more cunning and intelligent than we tend to give credit to. Instead of taking a nation in a loud and explicit manner, he works more quietly to erode it's underlying moral fabric. He seeks to tear down the family, biblical manhood/womanhood, and human sexuality to the point that it only marginally resembles God's good design and intended order. And when he's successful, crowds celebrate it. As the prophetic words of Isaiah ring out, "Woe to those who call evil good and good evil" (Isa. 5:20), they are just as true as the day they were spoken.

The devil is clever enough to work underneath these large pillars, putting smaller schemes and tactics in place to aid society in falling apart more quickly. For instance, one of the greatest spiritual and developmental threats for men today comes in the form of the social phenomenon of extended adolescence—a yearning to choose comfort above all things. When these two dynamics are considered together, men are too easily falling prey to a life without divine purpose. What a victory in the eyes of evil!

I'm not alone in suggesting this; rather, unexpectedly and most interestingly—a few outspoken voices in our contemporary culture wars have argued along similar grounds. Though these proclamations are not from those we would have predicted to speak out against such moral attacks. Yet their splinters of genuine reason have cut through the noise of the conversation. These are the voices of "the outsiders," as I like to refer to them.

And frankly, many of them are not followers of Jesus, nor are they trying to pretend to be. It's via their own moral intuition and reasoning that they recognize something is deeply wrong with how our society is speaking to men and helping them grow up.[4] I won't be shy about the fact that for every word spoken that's deemed praiseworthy, a warning must also follow in step. So many men are being shaped by these voices that we ought to discern where their wisdom is being sourced.

Rise of the Outsiders

In the classic Disney film *Peter Pan*, we meet an eternally youthful boy named Peter who lives in Neverland.[5] In this fantasy world, Peter is the leader of the lost boys, who battle against Captain Hook and his fellow pirates. However, things get interesting when the main characters, Michael, John, and Wendy, are whisked away one night from their London home by Peter and entrenched in his world. As the story unfolds, Wendy has growing feelings for Peter—which he could not reciprocate in his youthfulness—so she reminds her brothers they must return home to their parents in London and grow up as normal children.

Ultimately, Peter defeats Captain Hook and then returns Wendy and her brothers home. However, as the story comes to a close, Peter and the lost boys are just not ready to grow up, and instead of remaining in the real world, they return to Neverland to remain children forever. And herein lies the current issue at stake: Peter Pan may be a fictional character, but he's in the heart of far too many men in our society who refuse to grow up, take responsibility for their lives, and serve those around them—not the other way around—for the sake of God and their family.

While this message isn't preached in many churches, it *is* being addressed increasingly from those outside their walls. Somewhat ironically, like every bullhorn preacher at the corner of the street calling for repentance, these outsiders boldly speak to, coach, and motivate younger generations to awaken from their immature slumber. They are straight talkers, who don't hesitate to speak their mind regardless of social pressure or perception. Depending on whom you ask, a list of the most influential outsiders may include the likes of Jordan B. Peterson, Joe Rogan, Stoicism-influenced Ryan Holiday, former Navy seals David Goggins and Jocko Willink. And you won't find any of them pinned down by any tribe, group, or label. These guys are true outsiders, looking in on the Western church, American Evangelicalism, and its culture.

They don't share our Christian-ese verbiage or terms about manhood. Instead, they use common terms from the worlds of personal development, psychology, productivity, self-improvement, or self-help. And more often than not, their message comes with some explicit language and amusing stories before pivoting to reach a deeper level of vulnerable conversation. And men listen to them—like a mind-blowing amount. Joe Rogan alone has more than 14.5 million regular subscribers.[6] So, whether they acknowledge it or not, their voices carry weight in cultural debates and problems within Western society about manhood.

Peterson, himself, uses the tale of Peter Pan to contend that any putting off of maturity by men only accrues a greater cost than those who were willing to sacrifice their youthfulness.[7] He isn't wrong either. We (as men) all need to hear this message—in and outside the church. Peterson is in good company—as the likes of Henri Nouwen and Ronald Rolheiser have also acknowledged the dangers of remaining an "eternal boy," which robs us of the goodness of wisdom to be gained from growing up into spiritual adulthood.[8]

Unlike the latter authors and theologians, Peterson isn't a self-professed Christian—though he frequently integrates biblical narratives into his lectures. However, rather interestingly, he despises questions on his personal belief in God because they are often intended as traps or merely meant to affirm the interviewer's presuppositions.[9] I can empathize with his suspicion of those only looking for him to affirm, or deny, whether he's in their "tribe" or "side of the battle." We don't have to look far to recognize the deep wounds that can be caused within the church.

So, maybe, he's reading the room well—and wouldn't enjoy the religious mob waiting to throw insults and drown him in questions of doubt—if he stated that he's become a Christian. We've seen several public figures torn apart by fellow Christians after they proclaimed Jesus's name. Talk about the gross, friendly fire that can occur from inside the walls of the church once you've walked in. Maybe Peterson simply reckons there's more incentive to remain an outsider, both intellectually and physically. What a pitiful reality to consider about the state of our witness in the world.

Even in light of his stated hesitations about believers, Peterson has addressed pastors and churches on the topic of manhood. In July 2022, he uploaded a video to YouTube titled "Message to the Christian Churches," whereby he urged them to act on this issue within society, welcome young men into their churches, and help grow them into the best versions of themselves and the men that society needs.[10] What a fantastic idea! Even an outsider realizes the potential generational impact that would occur if the church took seriously its calling to raise boys into men.

Yet, all that to say, I'd argue Peterson is filled with a sense of false optimism. His push to drive men to the church isn't as meaningful or effective as he hopes. While genuine, the invitation only brings to the surface a greater tension in society—the average guy isn't interested in walking through the doors of a local church. Most people, not just men, don't have a high view of the church. And even if they were willing to attend, the men inside the church are often equally in a state of disappointment or resentment due to the lack of effort in helping them grow. As a result, men (in general) have tuned out pastors as their primary source of personal, spiritual, and relational development. It's been given away to these outsiders. And it leads to a vicious cycle that I've witnessed over and over again for the last decade.

The Road to Hell Is Paved with Good Intentions

As we explored in our opening chapter, everyone is influenced by some kind of wisdom—wisdom from above or wisdom from below. These sources of wisdom shape our desires, longings, and identity. Even those who have yet to realize they are drinking from a well filled with wisdom from below remain caught in its grip. Our perception of the wisdom that's influencing us can differ in reality from the kind which is truly guiding us. Many men would say they aren't formed by wisdom from below, while exercising it daily in their lives—as they cheat, hide, and live in the shadows. The key to discerning what kind of wisdom is guiding us is found in what spills out in our conversations and actions.

Whether we're influenced by wisdom from above or below, it will naturally compel us to invite others to follow the same wisdom we seek. These two sources of wisdom both call for men to surrender to them. Because these wisdoms—from below and above—preach their own gospel with two different ends. Whether it's explicit or not, these outsiders preach a gospel, and though each is unique, their message largely follows the self-help/improvement movements through the years. The difference now is that their tone is much louder, far more challenging, and direct as commentators. Another key feature of the outsider's gospel is the calling to suffer and rid ourselves of excuses for the sake of a better self tomorrow. Such a theme is clearly noted in the motivational works from former Navy Seal, David Goggins.[11]

And when thinking about our habits, our posture in life, and our relationships, we'd do well to consider Ryan Holiday, a best-selling author, who offers Stoic-inspired life advice—including his daily journal, *The Daily Stoic: 366 Meditations on Wisdom, Perseverance, and the Art of Living.*[12] In Christian circles, we call this a "devotional." The general sentiment that suffering produces endurance is rather difficult to argue with. The same is true of his encouragement for us to steep ourselves in the ancient Latin words, *memento mori*, meaning "remember death." Nothing about either of these works is blatantly anti-Christian from the surface, yet we also must more deeply consider the worldview attached to it.

Just as with every prior generation of the self-help movement, much of this content is grounded in what we call "*natural law* truths." Scripture speaks of the *natural law* as the source for why unbelievers can testify to certain moral truths, pursue good and beautiful things, and often live a "good life" (Rom. 2:14–15). When these outsiders speak about becoming the best version of yourself, manhood, or other cultural issues, they say, "This is just common sense."

They aren't wrong at all. Rather, it's spot-on (*theologically speaking*). You don't have to be a follower of Jesus to recognize that murder is wrong, a person with an XY chromosome is a male, enjoying meaningful friendships is immensely satisfying for our souls, or that practicing patience, kindness, or any other virtue is good and healthy for one's character. These truths testify to the existence of the *natural law* (think: design/order) and how we were intended to experience God's good creation and sense of living, as his image bearers.

However, let us return to our trustworthy old friend, St. Augustine, who wrote, "A good and true Christian should realize that truth belongs to his Lord, wherever it is found, gathering and acknowledging it, even in Pagan literature."[13] This is where our more modern phrase, "All truth is God's truth," stems from. So imagine in a fantasy world where I find myself alongside Augustine, Joe Rogan, and Jordan B. Peterson sitting around a firepit and talking about life. It would be okay and appropriate to applaud and praise Joe and Jordan wherever we (Augustine and myself) could. That's just the nature of engaging, healthy, and civil dialogue. It's a good thing to befriend those with different worldviews than our own. It's an opportunity to gain perspective and honor truth when it's spoken, no matter who it's from, whether it's these outsiders or not.

Though I would also expect that to be only one side of the conversation around the fire. Because, if we respect someone, we care enough to challenge him (and these outsiders certainly love that). Judging by the remaining half of Augustine's quote, he would stir things up. He continues saying, "But rejecting superstitious vanities and deploring and avoiding those who though they knew God did not glorify as God or give thanks but became enfeebled in their own thoughts and plunged their senseless minds into darkness."[14] Augustine doesn't mince his words, does he? We should honor truth when it's spoken, while investigating the source from which it comes. Anybody can speak the truth. Even in the Gospels, demons recognize the truth of who Jesus is. And these outsiders aren't that, nor are they speaking directly about the divinity of Christ, but *natural law* truths are grounded in *natural revelation*.

Augustine pushes us to wrestle with a deeper tension in consideration of these outsiders. Even when they speak into culture with a splinter of truth not preached in our churches, it doesn't mean they become our example or archetype for manhood. It doesn't mean these outsiders become our wise counsel, spiritual guide, or primary source of personal development. Even as we exhale from some deep belly laughs and are challenged by some of their content and podcasts, we must keep our guard up and be leery of how it is spiritually forming us.

In a fallen world, truth (and those who speak it) can be separated from the One that makes it true. We need to recognize that *natural-law* truths were never intended to be separated from our greater knowledge of and relationship with God. And neither should our spiritual formation.

I don't mean to be harsh, but the wisdom offered by these outsiders is more analogous to fool's gold than the real thing.[15] At first glance, it appears helpful and resourceful for our development. Yet we can't be so naïve to not analyze the well of wisdom these outsiders are drinking from. It's not until we take what they offer to the furthest degree that we realize how spiritually bankrupt it is. And that's because, when taken to its ultimate end, the message of suffering for the sake of self-mastery will eventually turn inward toward self-deception and self-worship. For many of these outsiders, their gospel of self-improvement will never bring us to meet the crucified Savior, nor will it clarify *why* we should push through the pain, suffering, and setbacks of life.

However, that's not to say these outsiders are against religion. That's simply not true. Peterson has adopted a more complicated take, which integrates a more abstract form of Christianity that situates the narrative of Scripture within a psychological framework. And in a way that illuminates how the *natural law* can guide our reasoning, Rogan has contended that our secular society comes at a significant cost and that we genuinely need a form of divine structuring from religion that helps uphold the sanctity of love and truth.[16] Many of the other outsiders may view religion favorably, but they don't speak on such. And herein lies the real issue—this is the furthest they can take their *message of self-mastery* because they haven't offered themselves to Jesus, surrendered their pride and will, and sought after true wisdom from above.

Their best intentions in discussing the complications and tragic state of manhood in our Western world are shallow in comparison to the rich depths Jesus calls us toward. Their vision may be virtue oriented, which is a good step forward in a culture void of truth and goodness, but that's not enough. A man's calling isn't fulfilled by merely providing a roof overhead, financial stability, or more opportunities for his children than he had. And you aren't necessarily a more remarkable man if you're doing all that while maintaining your workouts, balancing a hobby or two, and being at your kid's sports practices. These are all good, but if our vision of manhood is void of growing in greater likeness of Jesus and being immersed in the wisdom of God, then we've forsaken the highest aspect of our calling as a man.

My greatest fear for these outsiders (and those listening) isn't that they are completely failing as men—they aren't. They've spoken some solid words worth listening to—as natural law truths about culture. And I hope their message awakens some men from their deep, youthful slumber. However, as a pastor, I can't ignore the fact that the rise of these outsiders has also produced a subtle acceptance of a lesser form of manhood that's been stripped of its Divine origin.

So read this with your full attention. We should do the hard work of outgrowing our "Peter Pan" years. We ought to take responsibility for our lives. We should care about being the best husband and father and pushing ourselves to become the best version of ourselves. We must cultivate a virtuous character and seek to kill our ego and pride. Yet, if we don't do this hand in hand with God, taking refuge in him, and be Spirit-led in cultivating wisdom from above, then the old adage, "The road to hell is paved with good intentions," rings all too true.

When the Pattern of the World Looks Divine

The true mark of a good godly man starts with his relationship with God. From that fundamental relationship, our character is formed and godly wisdom is cultivated and then poured outward into our relationships and care for others. Our actions are a culmination of what lies beneath. And that's precisely why we cannot hand over our formation to those who aren't steeped in wisdom from above. I know the rise and popularity of these outsiders with Christian men stands on their frustration—that we aren't being challenged like men who desire to lead their families well in a world that's gone mad. But I promise—looking more and more to these outsiders isn't the counsel we need.

If we return to our core illustration about the wells of wisdom, it forces another uncomfortable conclusion. If the enemy's ways are often far more subtle and cunning than we give credit to, then we should be wary of the outsiders' gospel as just another proxy from the devil to block a revival of men pursuing God. Think about it—more than ever, men are reaching out for help and guidance. What would be the enemy's most effective strategy to block a revival of men coming to Christ? To offer them a counterfeit gospel of self-improvement that conveniently parallels a few biblical themes and spiritual practices—accountability, pride as a vice, responsibility, and suffering for the sake of growth. All while ignoring the most pressing existential crisis—our desperate need of God.

When outsiders reference Jesus's words as a helpful guide but sever them from his divinity, it's a grave error. One that someone only makes when they don't realize the wisdom they're being influenced by. And when the world's pattern looks so divine, its cunningness can only come from one source—and it's not God (2 Cor. 11:14). That doesn't mean we reject these outsiders; rather, the opposite. Embrace them and take Augustine's caution to heart: stay watchful of its source.

For all the content we digest daily or weekly, we must ask ourselves, *How is this shaping our thoughts, impulses, and values?*

How are these messages forming our heart and mind? We should listen in closely and honor the truth when it's spoken. Yet, in this confused, wayward world, we must also develop better discernment of its source. In Scripture, Paul calls us to have discernment for the ways in which we allow the world to take root in our minds (Rom. 12:1–2). Every day, we must decide what type of content our eyes will take in, what our ears will listen to, what our mind will store in memory, and, ultimately, what either leads us closer to God or further away from Him.

I recognize this all may be thought of as seeing the world in a narrow black-and-white framework—between what's clearly good and bad for our souls. But that couldn't be further from the truth. The whole point of this chapter is to find healthy discernment of what remains in the gray. I've heard people say, "Remember there's a lot of complexity in the gray." And that's true. But remember this too—acting as though there isn't a clear contrast to that which is good and evil will eventually cave to accepting any behavior in our lives and society at large.

And the church ought to be the place where we can sort it out wisely, learning to navigate the gray together. It should spur us on to sit around the fire, challenging one another on what is healthy and unhealthy for consumption. And it especially ought to be the place men should come to gain wisdom, friendship, work through addictions and brokenness, and find hope and healing. The church should be that for men—as God called it to be.

Reflection and Group Discussion Questions

1. What resources or content have you used to help build you up as a follower of Jesus, a husband, and a father? How have they helped you on your spiritual journey?

2. If you divided up that content by those who drink from the wisdom from above and below, how much of the content would you estimate comes from each?

3. What boundaries do you have in place for the content that may come from those that are influenced from wisdom from below?

4. How have you previously thought about the way content you consume shapes your thoughts and values? Why is it so vital now to put on the lens of the wisdom from above and below in interpreting your consumption?

5. Is there anything in your content consumption that you need to confess to a trusted group that is toxic for your spiritual life?

3

Spit You Out

"Appear to be what thou art, tear off thy masks. The church was never meant to be a masquerade."[1]
Charles Spurgeon

In the book of Revelation, Jesus commissions John in a vision to write letters to seven churches throughout Asia Minor, modern-day Turkey (1:4, 11). These letters, though brief, are densely packed with affirmation, encouragement, and warnings to be heeded and passed on to other local surrounding churches.[2] However, out of the seven letters, the church in Laodicea received the harshest rebuke of all the churches. Jesus calls out their lukewarm faith. They have become trusting of their wealth and resources over God himself. In their letter, Jesus also provides some spirited imagery to stir up some needed self-examination of where they really stand before God. Read this slowly, letting the weight of these words sink deeply into your soul:

> "I know your deeds,
> that you are neither cold nor hot.
> I wish you were either one or the other!
> So, because you are lukewarm—neither hot nor cold—
> I am about to spit you out of my mouth."
> (Rev. 3:15–16)

These words have echoed through the generations of time—starting in the first century in Laodicea—and are just as true for us here today. They arrive in the twenty-first century with the same stinging caution for churches and the believers that fill up their seats on any given Sunday. And like the Laodiceans, we all tend to tell ourselves stories that greater mirror a lie than the truth of our spiritual condition. We are all guilty of focusing on what can make us and our families more secure and protected in this depraved world. And we can do so, all while believing we are in the right, as we kneel before Jesus, only to realize we were never bowing before him at all but rather to a false god—one built by our own hands that reaffirms our comfort, reflection, security, and desired end.

So, as we look at this last piece of the cultural landscape forming us as men, we now turn inward by acknowledging and navigating the pride and hypocrisy that have nestled their way into the American church. And we do so by delving further into Jesus's words to the Laodiceans and grasping their historical context because it doesn't feel so different from our own. Like the Laodiceans, we too have made unworthy exchanges of God's best for our lives. Their story may just be the remedy to help lower our guards in this much-needed conversation, as we navigate our path forward in our calling to be wise, godly men.

The Beginning of Unworthy Exchanges

In a world that preaches ambition and self-reliance as distinguished virtues, Jesus turns such thinking on its head. The main challenge in hearing this is that we tend to get defensive about where the discussion might lead. But, even now, when we think about the virtues of a "real man" in the context of the West, the esteemed "self-made" man is sowed directly into the highest class of the American dream. We love stories of start-up companies and generational leaders who worked their hands to the bone, relying on substantial doses of caffeine and grit in the start-up phase to eventually raise their business to a place of remarkable growth and delegation of leadership.

Ambition, dedication, and success are not inherently wrong. Rather, they are the underpinnings of innovation. But a shadow side often hangs in these motivations. There's a plague which too frequently follows success—not merely in the wealth and resources acquired but about who we become along the way. If you don't know what I mean—just watch the film *The Founder*, the story of McDonald's, to recognize how unceasing ambition can so unmercifully decay one's character over time, as Ray Kroc so well demonstrates.[3] That's precisely the underlying warning Jesus is sending to the Laodicean church: In our increasing wealth, resources, and opportunity of self-reliance, *who* have we become devoted to, and whom do we trust? *What* is the source of our comfort and security?

This is the start of a conversation most of us admittedly approach with a sense of fear and trembling of entering. Because we intuitively recognize that Jesus isn't questioning nonbelievers on this but those who claim to follow the way of the crucified King. I also know that I'm probably not alone in imagining the pure terror of kneeling before the throne of God only to have Jesus look down and say,

"I know you.
Who you are and long to be.
Not what you hope others view you as.
I can see what your heart truly desires.
I know your actions—in the light and amid the dark.
And now, I will spit you out."

Who would ever desire this fate? I doubt the Laodicean Christians had any inklings of what lay waiting for them in the words of that letter. Yet, I wonder whether there were any outliers or counterweights at the church that tried to course-correct their church on a prior occasion. Or had they all so willingly blindfolded themselves and exchanged their trust in

God for their own hands? Unfortunately, the latter circumstance seems more likely.

As inhabitants of a notable ancient city, the Laodiceans found themselves amid the temptations of power, influence, great wealth, and resources—their city was famous for its fine black wool, exceptional medical center, and eye ointment.[4] However, the key to interpreting Jesus's words within their historical context is to recognize that Laodicea had no water supply of its own. It relied on the hot springs from the north and cold streams from the east. When they piped in water to the city from the northern hot springs, it often hadn't had time to cool and arrived lukewarm. It was also full of calcium deposits that often caused its drinkers to be sick and vomit.[5]

So Jesus's telling the Laodicean church to be hot, like the northern hot spring's healing properties, or even chilled, like the pure drinking water from the east, would have been better. But they were neither. They were as lukewarm as they came.

Though members of the Laodicean church could stroll into church in fine clothing, showcasing expensive jewelry, and secure their safety in investments, that wasn't what mattered in the eyes of God. Underneath all their self-reliance and security, they were nothing more than pitiful cultural Christians in name only—blinded by their deceit, poor in their spiritual well-being, and naked (fully exposed) in their shameless, self-dependent, twisted understanding of faith (Rev. 3:17–18). They weren't zealous or searching after God's heart because they were already satisfied by the work of their own hands.

Perhaps you recognize that you're standing in the same place as the Laodiceans—your true measure of trust and fulfillment has become self-driven. It may be the number in your bank account, the size of your house, the number of employees who work for you, or the networking connections that make you feel important, worthy, and a notch above everyone else. Maybe, instead of taking comfort and security in God, you secretly hold greater stock in the perception that you're a good, hardworking man or a godly kind of man at church on Sundays.

But if we take away anything from this opening discussion on Jesus's warning to the Laodicean church, remember this: We can always fool the world, our coworkers, and even our family and friends, but not Jesus. Our outward appearances and social status mean little to the heart of Jesus. And God knows every unworthy exchange we are making, instead of embracing his way of life. God already knows our deepest source of fulfillment, security, and identity. In fact, he knows us better than we even know ourselves (Ps. 139:1–4). Let that reality settle in—for two thousand years not a single soul has sat in God's house and fooled him about where they place their trust and security, even if they claim to bear his name.

Whitewashed Tombs

Jesus never disguised his anger for those pretending to stand for him. In tune with his rebuke of the Laodicean church, Jesus saved his most calculated and harsh words for the scribes and Pharisees. Throughout the gospel story, Jesus steadily increases his accusations against the self-serving hypocrites until he launches an all-out verbal takedown of them toward the end of his life, as described in Matthew 23. Jesus calls them out for their false righteousness, hypocritical living, spiritual blindness, lack of concern for justice and mercy, unceasing pride, and their endless craving for notoriety before others.

To pour gasoline on the fire, Jesus used a picture-perfect metaphor to illuminate his charges against them, describing these religious leaders as "whitewashed tombs." While they outwardly appear to look good and beautiful to the eye, inwardly they are full of filth and rotting bones of the dead (Matt. 23:27–28). Jesus has an issue with people who lie to themselves and others that they are following after God's heart when they secretly have no desire to please him. It's his message to the Laodiceans and the Pharisees, but it still calls out to us today.

Though it would be more comfortable to sweep this conversation under the rug and declare, "We aren't like them," I would challenge each of us to avoid that immediate denial and admit that we, too, can be full of hypocrisy. We too have the capacity to put on a mask and pretend. Because far too often we fall prey to the same traps. Even the most sold-out, faithful man of God will always have a subtle fleshly pull that tempts him to succumb to the same pitfalls as the Pharisees. Each of us has a desire to be seen and known as a "good guy" who commands respect and a nod of the cap from others, while we're walking around the church. Or maybe, it's at the mall or on the ball fields. We are broken people doing broken things. Yet there's also a difference between seeking affirmation as a "people pleaser" and living a double spiritual life.

Becoming a whitewashed tomb begins with a desire for others to view us as a genuine follower of Jesus, while privately withholding our surrender to God. It's holding up a mask in front of others to disguise our waywardness. As a result, we allow wisdom from below to grow in the shadows of our soul, all while claiming that we walk in the light of wisdom from above. It's claiming to be surrendered to Jesus when our life mirrors apathy, numbness, and the vices of false idols.

To be blunt, I think it's fair to say too many men in our churches, Bible studies, and community groups are nothing more than whitewashed tombs. Their lives are not wholly devoted to God but greater marked by hell than heaven. Where they claim to have found freedom in Jesus, they remain shackled to their addictions, spiritual blindness, and unbridled pride. I recognize the face, the hidden shame, of these modern whitewashed tombs because I was one of them.

For years, I was a committed church attender, took notes and completed all my sermon fill-ins, and participated in service projects when I could. Yet, the truth is, I refused to sacrifice my porn addiction to God. I didn't read the Word to grow closer in intimacy with God but for the sake of gaining factual knowledge that I could readily expound upon in conversation. If I'm transparent, the Bible was just my primary source of behavior modification—keeping my worst impulses at bay. It was a means of shaming myself into more controlled behavior. I felt the excruciating weight of hypocrisy when I went to a Baptist college and felt so incredibly lonely. For whatever reason, I thought it was better for others to believe I was the "good Christian guy," when internally I was nothing more than an isolated, broken, and struggling young man.

It's why I'm more keenly aware of the masks we can all put on and the words we can hide behind on a Sunday morning. I get it; I was there, too, and it's a miserable place. As Spurgeon reminded us in the opening of this chapter, the church is not a masquerade, but it too quickly can resemble one. Too frequently, we don't desire to confront this issue within the local church because it can itself get too busy listening to and using methodologies more aligned with wisdom from below.[6]

I don't wholly blame the individual on this matter. We are a society driven by consumerism and individualism, which has crept its way into the local church. I'm terrified that our modern church culture has produced millions of whitewashed tombs. It's not difficult to trace the abundance of cultural Christians born from the spiritual shallowness of the Christian self-help train and seeker-sensitive church growth movement of the late 90s and early 2000s. Though, don't be too hasty to mistake this as a past trend. Its reign is not over. We are still reeling from its consequences and its seeds that were planted in the current generation of celebrity pastors and attraction-based megachurches.

Throughout North America, we've made the bar so low in our churches for participating in discipleship. If we show up on Sunday, maybe a small group during the week, the perception is we have a thriving relationship with Jesus. But we both know we can just go through the motions, treating our actions as mere tasks without longing for the heart of God and intimacy with him. The American church isn't crumbling because attendance is declining year over year but rather because it has not prioritized cultivating and conforming its members into Christ's image via discipleship and spiritual formation practices.[7] If we claim we desire for men to grow into their calling, we must first ask: How is the inner world of a man becoming like the inner being of Jesus by the power of the Holy Spirit?[8]

It's a question of obedience before God that should shake each one of us to the core. Like Jesus's words to the Laodiceans, it should pierce our comfortable faith and consumerism mentality. The point of this book is to challenge and convict our hearts and minds (worldview) before God.

So let us openly acknowledge it: For far too many men, it has become easy and acceptable to sit on the sidelines regarding their spiritual formation and service within the church. And it's because we allowed the situation to occur. Remaining on the sidelines produces spiritual complacency, which eventually turns toward the lack of prioritization of faith. It leads to Sunday becoming a checkbox—walking in without taking off our mask and neither offering ourselves for who we really are upon God's alter.

No one sets out to become a whitewashed tomb, but it's a central facet of the cultural landscape within the church for men. Unfortunately, we aren't quite done yet. There's one more unworthy exchange men face in the church today, which needs to be mentioned: Men are slowing their pursuit of God, even landing themselves in lukewarm territory, by entangling themselves in a futile state of frustration over culture and politics.

A Citizen Between Two Kingdoms

Like most in our day, I have often muttered to myself, *How could this world grow more absurd and chaotic than it already is?* Then, like clockwork, I turn on the news, and the answer lies before me. I no longer watch mainstream news—not to isolate myself from such realities but due to the unceasing frustration that grows within myself as I watch all the various ways our world is currently falling apart at the seams.

I, too, understand why so many guys are concerned about the state of our country. We live in a highly chaotic time where totalitarian governments invade neighboring nations, terrorists attack rock concerts, and children are shot in road-rage incidents. Tampons are placed in elementary school bathrooms for boys, and marches are held for human rights—all while discarding blameless unborn babies like it was nothing. As Christians, we find ourselves in a difficult position to navigate all the madness of our culture and politics wisely.

Yet nothing about our cultural situation is a new phenomenon. This has always been true for the people of God. Since the fall, the nations have raged against God and his people. Scripture is filled with stories of God's people enduring evil kings and imperial powers. From Israel's enslavement in Egypt to seventy years in Babylonian captivity, not to mention the birth of the church amid Roman exploitation and persecution, cultural opposition has always risen in each age.[9]

So we must take heart and recognize our place in God's greater story as sojourners that will never call this world our home or find comfort in it (Phil. 3:20; 1 Pet. 2:11). That doesn't mean we retreat to the mountains from our decaying society. Rather, the opposite is needed. Given our increasingly secular society, we must take our role as faithful witnesses more seriously than ever. Our public squares are the battlegrounds for false gods, each vying for greater cultural power, influence, and worship.[10] Even with that acknowledgment, it's not our responsibility to win any cultural or political battle for Jesus.

Just as Jesus ushered in the kingdom under the rule of the Roman Empire, our sacred calling is to stand as God's representatives amid our unrepentant, idolatrous culture and increasingly turbulent state of affairs. Regardless of who wields the power of the Oval Office, it doesn't change the reality that Christ still sits on his throne. Our heavenly allegiance and citizenship triumph over any form of earthly citizenship (Phil. 3:20). We ought to be the best kind of citizens, since God calls us to uphold goodness, justice, and truth in our private and public spheres of life. Yet we must take the story of God's people seriously: We are called to commit our lives and homes to the Lord, but the same is not required of this country.

Our true victory isn't to reverse the descent of immorality which has overtaken society but to save souls and be a signpost to the gospel in the trenches of the spiritual war within it. As American Christians, we tend to be sensitive to this notion, clamming up in suspicion that it sounds unpatriotic. However, our biblical worldview calls for us to be wise and discerning that whoever leads our government is neither our Savior nor our standard for moral conduct. That's reserved for Christ, alone.

Do I pray that we find ourselves in the ideal situation that those in political offices have surrendered their life to Christ? Of course, especially for my kid's sake! Their temporary influence can lead to good and just policies for our society—which can incline us to be a more virtuous society. All that is, indeed, good. Yet we mustn't fool ourselves in a place of naivete to believe those laws will produce followers of Jesus. We can pay attention to politics, but we must keep our eyes fixed upon the greater spiritual battle which rages on—in our country, states, cities, neighborhoods, and homes.

We must become more committed to sharing the gospel with power and tenacity that cut through any cultural challenge or political rhetoric this world offers. We must learn to interweave and prioritize the ways of Jesus in any conversation on culture and politics. To mix up these priorities is the same as falsely elevating materialism and wealth; both displease God. Each is an unworthy exchange, leading us astray and to replace God as our main commitment and priority.

I fear that too many dinner tables have become a common place for passionate conversations around culture and politics rather than speaking of God's goodness and faithfulness. Our children are overhearing it and will naturally believe these priorities matter more than topics that are eternally significant. So, again, we return to the letter to the Laodiceans, where Jesus says he stands at their door, knocking, waiting to be let in to enjoy a meal together (Rev. 3:20). How would you respond? And let me question each of us on this too—if we did let him in, what do we believe Jesus would want to talk about with our families? Because that's how we, as the leaders of our households, should also be leading the conversation around the table each day.

Come to the Table

The Laodiceans had their issues—and not the type anyone could easily sweep under the rug. Jesus spoke harshly with them because their level of disobedience demanded it. Yet God had not abandoned them either, even as he proclaimed how rotten they had become. Jesus reminded them that he corrects and disciplines all those he loves so that they may repent and return to passionately pursuing him with all their heart, mind, and soul (Rev. 3:19). More than that, Jesus asks them to invite him in for a meal and says he will even bring everything for them. Jesus wants us at the table with him so that we can live the most flourishing life by abiding in him. Only God can provide that for us—not a better political state.

As it often is with Jesus's rebukes throughout the Gospels, they tend to speak to us as much as his original audience. For each of us (myself included), Jesus's words continue to speak directly to our hearts today. That's because Jesus meets us in our brokenness and messes of life. We are never too far gone in our hypocrisy or our waywardness to be rescued by God. And not just once, but he will do it again and again because we are not just another disposable problem for him. Like every good and loving Father, God disciplines us *so that* we may grow into the man, husband, father, and friend we were called to become (Prov. 3:11–12; John 15:1–7).

He's the Good Shepherd who tracks down the one lost sheep so all can come home to their Father (Matt. 18:10–14; Luke 15:1–7). Maybe you were once zealous after him, constantly reading your Bible and meditating on its truths, but now you're empty, tired, and void of passion for him. Maybe you've placed far too much faith in the things of this world and its leaders. Maybe you walk into church every Sunday knowing you're unwilling to sacrifice your addictions and vices for him. Or perhaps you haven't asked him into your life at all, while acting as though you have.

Ask Jesus in so that he can sit with you. Opening the door for God is the only way to find true freedom and peace. So may we always be reminded that Jesus stands at the front of our home:

Invite him in.
Welcome him to the table.
Talk with him.
Let him teach you.
Encourage you.
And learn to depend on him.
Because Jesus sustains us, not our conditions.
He's already brought everything we need.

Reflection and Group Discussion Questions

1. How do you think the Laodiceans felt when they heard that letter from Jesus being read to them? As you read Revelation 3:14–22, how do you feel?

2. Did you naturally make the connection between the Laodiceans and the Pharisees as whitewashed tombs? How have you struggled with hypocrisy or self-reliance in your walk with God?

3. Have you felt overwhelmed by the issues within culture for yourself, your kids, or your grandkids? What healthy steps can we take to have the conversation about Jesus?

4. Read John 15:1–16. How has God disciplined or intentionally pruned you in your walk with him? How did you feel afterward?

5. Is there an area of your life now that you need to surrender to him?

4

Image Bearer

"The most important thing in your life
is not what you do; it's who you become.
That's what you'll take into eternity."[1]
Dallas Willard

You were created in the image of God. Through every high and low, from mountaintops to the desert and wilderness and the deep valley experiences of life, there is nothing we can do to change that reality. We could plunge headfirst into a pleasure-driven hedonistic lifestyle, consumed neck-deep in addiction, and break every one of the Ten Commandments. Yet that name "image bearer" remains bestowed upon you. And held within that name is also our divine calling and identity as a human person, carved out in the likeness and reflection of God.[2] No amount of sin can deface that.[3] Even when we try, we can't outrun the truth of *who* we are.

Throughout Scripture, the use of *images* is important—more than we might even realize. From it being a designator of humanity in reflection of God to the second commandment, not to make any "graven image" (Exod. 20:4 KJV), all the way to Jesus Christ, described as the true image of God himself (Gen. 1:27; Exod. 20:4–6; Eph. 4:24; Col. 1:15). Yet, like the way of wisdom from *above* and *below*, the same is true for how *the image* is depicted in Scripture. We can choose to grow in greater reflection of Jesus or, instead, choose to mirror a perversely inverted image of an idol we willingly worship.[4]

But to understand our place in this world, we must venture further into the richness of the biblical story and the fullness of what it means to be conformed to the image of Jesus. To help us wrestle through what it means to be an image bearer, let us travel back to the ancient Near Eastern world, then return to the first century and the world of the New Testament.

Ancient Myths and Statues of the Gods

Every man has an origin story. While it can be challenging, it is worthwhile to retrace our beginnings because, whether we acknowledge it or not, it has fundamentally shaped who we are as men. We don't get to choose the place or time of when we come into this world, who our parents will be, or their condition and readiness for parenthood. And to add another layer of complexity, when we do arrive, we enter a world with its own significant moments of history. It doesn't revolve around us; we are brought into its greater story. Each of these facets of life helps us grasp our sense of *who* we believe we are, our identity in the world, because they combine to tell us about our perceived role within it.

However, people can interpret the overarching story of the world differently and, thus, raise their children to experience and live in the world to match that perception. Our upbringing and worldview impact our dreams, goals, values, even our perceived worthiness of self, and how we ought to carry ourselves before others. The story we're told of *who* we are supposed to be in this world shapes the men we become (*for better or worse*). If we returned to the ancient Near Eastern world, say Mesopotamia, we'd recognize this truth more fully. The stories we tell about our beginnings influence what we believe about ourselves.

Imagine trying to grasp your place in the world after hearing the story of the *Enuma elish*. In this creation myth, we meet the young and powerful god, Marduk, who wars against the ocean goddess and leader of the old gods, Taimat, and violently defeats her in battle.[5] Marduk then takes her corpse (described as a great dragon surrounded by seas), splitting it in two—creating the heavens out of her upper half and forming the earth below with her lower half. The other primordial gods look upon as these events unfold and declare him "the king of heaven and earth."[6] But Marduk desires a place where he can rule from the earth and has the other gods build his capital city, Babylon, complete with his temple to reside in and be worshipped. The other gods are also given temples so they too can move back and forth between heaven and earth.

However, not all is totally complete. After finishing Babylon, Marduk concedes that the gods should not do any further work. So he slaughters another rival evil god, Qingui, and out of his blood, Marduk brings humanity into existence for the sole purpose of serving the burdensome needs of the gods.[7] Humans were created as an afterthought, made to be enslaved people for the gods' convenience and enjoyment.[8] No inherent worth, dignity, or true calling in life. There's an intentional division between the gods and humans because of such perceived inherent value. As we will see, the heart of the one true God is so different.

However, the *Enuma elish* was widely influential in the Neo-Babylonian Empire of the seventh and sixth centuries BC.[9] Their whole society and political order were modeled after the likeness and traits of their gods. Accordingly, each new year, the human king of Babylon would participate in a ritual before the statue of Marduk to connect his divine power to the kings, marking their rulership as interconnected.[10] That's how deeply formative these myths were in ancient culture and civilization. Less has changed than we might think. Their world revolved around the gods in their temples, while now those same demons (in newer form) vie for our attention and command us to make sacrifices at their altars in different ways (Deut. 32:17; 1 Cor. 10:22).[11]

Before we discuss the biblical story, let's briefly turn southwest toward ancient Egypt. Amid its desert sand and pyramids, there's an intriguing view of the pharaohs that forms a closer parallel with our Western imaginations. Though the Babylonian *Enuma elish* painted a bleak picture of humanity, many ancient Egyptian texts (particularly 1500–101 BC) reference the pharoah, the royal king, as distinct from other humans. They were designated as the sons of gods, divine in nature and able to rule in their place.[12] More specifically, the lineage of pharaohs were cited as "the living image of god" and considered like a breathing statue of the sun god, Re—the national deity of Egypt.[13] It was then customary for rulers in the ancient Near East, including pharaohs, to erect statues, or icons, of themselves at the corners of their territories to signify their divine sovereignty and rulership over the land and its people.[14]

So, why have I gone to painstaking lengths to retell an ancient creation myth and describe how kings and pharaohs were notably elevated above ordinary people as divine images? Well, these pagan gods and stories were the cultural backdrop surrounding the writing of Genesis, and they will undoubtedly help us grasp just how radically different the biblical story (and its worldview) is in light of the ancient world.

A Story of Creation and Redemption That Rivals the False Gods

Scripture wasn't written in a cultural vacuum, void of understanding the outside world of pagan gods and creation myths. In fact, there's a whole academic field devoted to grasping the parallels of ancient Near Eastern texts and their relation to the Hebrew Scriptures. It's fascinating, and it's worth checking out a few main works in the field.[15] But now, as we dive into Scripture's creation narrative, try to place yourself within the ancient world by taking off your twenty-first-century lens.

In the opening creation story in the book of Genesis, God speaks the cosmos into existence and works for days to bring forth light to separate the darkness, the sky, oceans, land and vegetation, sun, stars, and moon. He also fills his creation with animals in the air and seas (Gen. 1:1–24). On the sixth day, God creates the animals of the land and then turns his attention toward what will be the focal point of his creation—Adam and Eve (humanity), made in his own likeness and image. He commands them to be fruitful, multiply, and rule over God's creation (Gen. 1:26–28). God looked at everything and said that "it was good"—not complete or finished, for that was humanity's task. On the seventh day he rested (Gen. 2:1–2).

God had built a cosmic temple, a sanctuary and garden filled with awe, beauty, and his glory on full display. It was a place where God and his people could dwell together. We are bestowed with a God-given identity as image bearers, unique to all other creatures in the cosmos.[16] God didn't need a statue—we were his images on earth—complexly fashioned with a physical body, soul/mind, desires, emotions, will, and so much more.

Each of us is seen as divine royalty with inherent dignity, respect, and honor. This beautifully ordered world was designed for our enjoyment and cultivation, to care for and rule over.[17] We were invited into an intimate, dependent friendship with God so we could learn to mirror his holy character and wisdom from above and reflect the ways of our Creator. We were to be God's family, not coerced into serving his every need (he needs nothing from us), but to rejoice and reign with a grateful, indebted heart that offers praise and glory for his goodness.

The garden of Eden was meant to be our home, and all its land was a sacred temple that reflected what the Hebrew prophets called *shalom*—a state of true human flourishing, where all things are the way they ought to be.[18] On the horizon was excitement, adventure, creativity, culture, and world-building—what scholars call the "cultural mandate."

However, the flourishing world of Genesis 1 came crashing down when Adam and Eve ate from the tree of the knowledge of good and evil. They were lured in by the serpent's tongue, but the driving force of their decision to sin was their pride (Gen. 3:1–6). Their disobedience to God resulted in banishment from Eden and introduced chaos, corruption, and death to the human experience and the rest of creation (*the curse*) (Gen. 3:14–19). Our once natural knowledge and relationship with God no longer exists. In the depths of his grace, God didn't abolish us as his image bearers or dismiss us from our task to fill and subdue. Now, instead of pursuing the development of the earth in a godly manner, we inherently do so by the power and wisdom from below, drawing upon its power in an abusive, subversive, and oppressive manner for our gain and glory.[19]

We are born sinners craving wayward desires in a profoundly broken world (Eph. 2:1–3). But, even in our state of sin and rebellion, God remained faithful and sought a people of his own to reflect his character and calling for humanity. God yearned for an earthly kingdom. So the creation mandate is recommissioned to Noah, but, unfortunately, he too soon fails (Gen. 9:7, 20–27). And then we meet Abraham, with whom God makes a covenant to build a great nation through his linage in the land of Canaan and to fulfill the mandate of multiplying and cultivating the earth for his glory (Gen. 12:1–3). This is the birth of the people of Israel, and through slavery in Egypt, forty years of wandering in the desert, and the rest of the Old Testament, God is committed to Israel as his covenantal people.

Like Adam and Eve in the garden, Israel was to represent God as his image bearers on earth, and to be a holy nation/

kingdom that ruled in his name. As a light to the world, they were meant to represent God's righteousness and proper way of life to the pagan nations (Exod. 19:4–6; Deut. 4:6–8). But, unlike in Eden, God couldn't freely dwell with his people because of the unholy state of the world, so he commanded them to build the tabernacle (a mobile tent-like temple), and later a permanent temple in Jerusalem (Exod. 25:1–40:38; Dan. 9:25). They would offer animals as sacrifices to atone for their sin. Israel should have responded with appreciation and obedience by following God's laws. But history would repeat itself again, and they, too, were lured away by idol worship, unfaithfulness, restlessness, and destructive rulership.

However, redemption would come in due time. It was long prophesied that a Messiah would come to take on our transgressions and to make our crooked paths straight (Isa. 42:1, 16; 53:5–6). Though our story begins with a rather quick descent that seemed impossible to slow or remedy, our story and calling doesn't end in despair. Yet our story and calling don't end in despair. Rescue and restoration were near and to be accomplished by the hands of God himself.

Redemption Day

Everything changed at the dawn of the first century. In a poor farming town named Bethlehem, the Son of God was born. God became incarnate to walk the earth and redeem us; Jesus of Nazareth, the God-man, arrived to fulfill all the promises and prophesies in the Old Testament (Gen. 3:15; Isa. 7:13–14; 11:2–9; 53:5; Dan. 2:44; Col. 1:15). He came to bring order and salvation to a world engulfed in chaos and disorder. In *How God Became King*, N. T Wright delivers an excellent summary of his mission, "In Jesus, Israel's God had become present, had become human, had come to live amidst his people, to set up his kingdom, to take upon himself the full horror of their plight, and to bring about his long-awaited world."[20]

Throughout his life and ministry, Jesus taught us of God's ways, wisdom from *above*, and what it means to be truly human. He perfectly reflected God in his humanity (Col. 1:15). Even though he could have remained in heaven, he made himself lowly, clothed himself in grace and humility—to the point of death—for our sake.

The only possible path to restoring humanity's calling and relationship with God—to atone for our deadly, idolatrous, sinful ways of life—would take a God-sized sacrifice. Though it would include public rejection, humiliation, and torture, Jesus demonstrated perfect obedience to his Father and sought to bring humanity back from the grips of estrangement with God.[21] And on a hillside in Jerusalem called Golgotha—Place of the Skull—with a crowd of his followers, Jewish leaders, and Romans, Jesus was crucified and took upon himself the sin of the world (John 19:17–22). Yet that wasn't the end. After three days, Jesus rose from the dead, defeating death, sin, and the power and plan of Satan.

Jesus would walk around for forty more days before returning to heaven to sit upon his Father's throne. But before he ascends to heaven, he calls over his disciples and commissions them to go out into all the world (from Jerusalem to the ends of the earth) and make disciples—to baptize and teach them wisdom from *above* and the ways of the one true God. The family of God, the church—not a nation—will be his divine representatives that embody his rule and reign. This is the sacred calling for those in his kingdom—that we reflect the holiness of God and be a light that can cut through every part of this dark and wayward world. Contra to the rival gods, the true God invites us into his story because he always intended for us to be intricately involved in it.

Jesus invites us to carry out our true calling—to grow in intimacy and wisdom with God so we may best serve as his presence, reflection, and representative for all we encounter. It's an invitation to grow in holiness through the work of the Holy Spirit and conform to the image of Christ (Rom. 8:28–29). When we trust in Jesus's work on the cross, we become united with it, indwelt by the Holy Spirit, and empowered to live out our true calling, as an image bearer of God—created to serve and rule in his name.

To Whose Image Will You Be Conformed?

Our lives are intertwined with God's unfolding story in the world. Yes, Jesus already came two thousand years ago to die for us, but it's now our turn to embrace his calling for us by growing further into his image, not our own. Throughout the rest of this book, we will walk the path of spiritual formation to become the man God has called us to be. We will dive into the ways of Jesus, his spiritual practices and habits, and discuss the importance of committing to daily die to ourself for the sake of God and those who surround us in life. I want each of us to become the husband, dad, and friend God created us to be. Are you ready for that?

Now that we've navigated through the cultural landscape at work to shape us as men, it comes down to a commitment only each of us can personally make. Not your wife, nor your kids, parents, friends, or anyone else. Are you ready to lay down your preconceived notions of what it means to be a man—your ambition, hopes, dreams, and vision of your life—and instead, take up God's way? Seriously, if you aren't ready to say yes, then I don't want you to continue reading this book filled with self-deception and a misaligned heart between you and God. This world doesn't need another whitewashed tomb.

From the start, Jesus was honest with his followers when he said to his disciples, "Whoever wants to be my disciple must deny themselves and take up their cross and follow me. For whoever wants to save their life will lose it, but whoever loses their life for me will find it" (Matt. 16:24–25). From our innermost private self—our thoughts, imagination, emotions, character, and habits—to our outward actions, roles, and responsibilities with our families and strangers alike, Jesus is asking us to surrender our ways for his so that we can learn to live as God intended.

As we move on to part 2, "The Man You're Called to Be," let's pray for our time ahead—that we each seek after the heart of God as men who desperately need to find him. The forthcoming chapters aren't easy and are potentially full of pain, hurt, and wounds we've pushed down for far too long. But hear this: With each sphere of life that we will be navigating through, we will have an opportunity to open our palms, turn them over, and surrender it to Jesus—so we can deepen our trust in him and be further molded into his character and image.

Before closing this chapter, pray through the following questions and write down your responses:

How would you describe a godly man?

What does his character look like?

What are his daily priorities?

What does his community of friends look like?

What does he do with the influence and power he holds?

Reflection and Group Discussion Questions

1. How do you define being a man, and what or who has most influenced your definition of such?

2. How does your faith shape your view of manhood, your role, and your responsibilities?

3. During this season of life, how would you evaluate yourself as a man? In which areas of your manhood are you succeeding? Which areas need improvement?

4. What are some ways you have sought to intentionally grow as a man, individually or alongside others?

5. How does your community either help or hurt your growth?

Part 2

The Man You're Called to Be

5

When You Look at Your Father

"The farther I run away from the place where God dwells, the less I am able to hear the voice that calls me Beloved, and the less I hear that voice, the more entangled I become in the manipulations and power games of the world."[1]

Henri Nouwen

In the months before my son, Noah, was born, I would catch myself in deep ruminating thought cycles about my existence and eventual death. Having a child is one of the most significant experiences in life because it beckons us to accept that our time is eclipsing, while theirs is beginning. We recognize that our son or daughter will soon look up to us. And that dawning truth stirs in us a new perspective on life, death, and everything in between. During those difficult months, I wrestled through a series of difficult, often negative, thoughts that traced along these lines:

Who indeed is the man my son will be looking up at?

Am I ready to have a son in my own image?

What if I'm not good enough?

What if I become a source of pain and mistrust for him?

What if I pass on the same kind of wounds I hold because of my father?

I wish I had known then that I didn't need to be drowning in the fear of passing on my shortcomings, sins, and wounds. What I needed in the greatest depths of my soul was to turn my attention and learn to abide in, trust, and be loved by my good heavenly Father. Today, I recognize more clearly than ever that God always intended it to be this way.

My deepest longing in my heart is that when my kids lift their heads to look at me they see through me to their perfect Father, who intimately knows, cares, and loves them in ways I only wish that I could. And this isn't to downplay my role or importance in their lives. It's the opposite. Rather, it's to uphold the truth that I was first loved by God, even before my own parents, and when I wholly accept that, I can best pour out a good Father's love to my family, friends, and community.

And that's why this is the starting place for every good and faithful man.

A Good Father and Two Lost Sons

One of the most famous parables in Scripture is that of the prodigal son, a story of a long-lost son's return home after squandering his inheritance on prostitutes and other sources of debauchery (Luke 15:11–32). You've probably heard it referenced when someone who's struggled with addiction, or put themselves through hell in other ways, comes to know Jesus and his story is celebrated as a homecoming akin to the prodigal son. For such a reason, people tend to interpret the most important lesson of this parable to be a story of repentance and those who need to return home to God after a season of empty pursuits. Or they look at the older brother's struggle as a self-righteous legalist and one's need to better understand the heart of grace. However, it's crucial to recognize that neither the wayward son nor the older self-righteous brother is the main focus of this parable; it's the heart and response of the good father.[2]

You see, both sons are lost in different ways. Obviously, the younger is estranged from his father in pursuit of wild indulgences. But, at the same time, the older brother who remained dutifully at home is also revealed to be spiritually bankrupt.[3] He may be on top of all his responsibilities of his father's property, but he accomplishes them with a self-serving motive. However, in handling this parable's meaning, it's important to recognize the possible interpretive dangers of solely tracing it through the vantage point of the sons. Typically, this is done by rabbit trailing down a path of self-projection onto either of the sons' journey, or characteristics. Such an approach, in general, leads one too easily to stay on the ground floor of the parable and neglect climbing up to see the forest from the trees in terms of the critical point it's making. So, instead, let's turn this into an exercise together. Grab your Bible and turn to Luke 15:11–32. Now read the parable through the father's lens, noting his response to both his sons.

What did you notice about the father? I'll tell you what I see: He's the one who took the *first* step in meeting both his sons in their messes. Look at verse 20; the father first sees his young prodigal son's return. The father drops everything and just sprints towards him, running as quickly as he possibly can with arms wide open to embrace his tattered, filthy, and foul-smelling son. And what does his father do when the eldest brother is standing bitter outside the house, spitefully rejecting his younger brother's welcome home? He doesn't get annoyed but, again, takes the *first* step to walk outside to comfort him, reminding him that he doesn't take for granted his faithfulness and loyalty (vv. 28–32). And what does this good father remind each of his sons amid their rejection of him? They are his beloved sons—worthy of his love, absolute best, resources, and sacrifice (vv. 22–24, 31).

As we read this parable, it can be relatively easy to find ourselves amid this story, my friends. You may be hiding in your failure and shame, but he still calls you his son. You may be covered in every bit of sin, but he's willing to meet you in the darkness of it. You may have fallen on hard times, but he's in the rescue and restoration business. You may have rejected him and walked away from your faith, and he's waiting for you to come home. And right now, you may be on the journey home like the younger brother, and he's filled with joy, running toward you. Or perhaps you're struggling with anger, lingering outside the homecoming party with the self-righteous legalistic older brother, but his grace and gentleness will come for you.

No matter where you are, you have a good Father who has taken the *first* step, and he's ready for you to learn the depths of his love. That's why Jesus died for us, so we too can call God "Abba, Father" (Rom. 8:15; Gal. 4:6). Our heavenly Father doesn't immediately cast us away when we dishonor him. Instead, he uses our mistakes as an opportunity to invite us into a deeper relationship with him, so that we may better understand his heart.

I recognize there can be pain in reading these lines above. Some of us have never had an earthly father that resembles this parable's good father. That's a heartbreaking reality for a lot of men. Unfortunately, too many of us grew up in broken homes and now carry a burden of pain we didn't ask for. We live in a fatherless generation. So maybe your father never stood outside the front door, waiting with his eyes peeled, hoping to get a glimpse of you walking home. Perhaps he never ran to you because he wasn't home at all; maybe he left and abandoned you when you were young. Or your parents split up, and the idea of a present father who pursues you is something *other* friends get to have but not *you*. I know the hurt that lies within these wounds well.

Yet, here's the thing—even those with the most committed, involved, and present fathers still have wounds to heal from theirs. No earthly father is perfect, nor were they intended to meet us in the same way our heavenly Father does. That's why we were always meant to see God as our perfect Father.

The Father Who Is—and I Was Never Intended to Be

By examining the father's heart toward his lost sons in the parable, we also get a glimpse of the character of our heavenly Father, who's ready to embrace us in the same way.[4] And likewise, as Jesus is a perfect human reflection of the Father, we, too, are called to grow into his character. But, to do that well, we must spend time with him, growing in our understanding of his heart, character, and love. We must learn to slowly unwind our assumptions about God as our Father and come to him each morning, saying, *I need you to sit with me today, teach me, and help me grow into the man that reflects who you are.* The truth of the matter is, that's exactly how it was supposed to be all along.

We weren't meant to have an experience of earthly fathers who could so quickly become consumed by their own shortcomings. It wasn't meant to be the case that I can only count a handful of my friends' parents who stayed together. We weren't meant to be in situations as children where we can't comprehend, feel, or hear the love of our father. But we live in the consequences of a sinful world, filled with broken people and homes, where its pain can be felt for generations—including how we relate to God. It's difficult not to project our experiences of our earthly father onto God himself. If your earthly father has been untrustworthy, unpredictable, or distant, it can be a struggle not to assume that must be true of our heavenly Father. Suppose you grew up with a father who was prone to rage, rigidness, and lacked empathy or support. It's hard not to expect those experiences from God, particularly in moments of life that bring us back to those emotions we felt with our earthly father.

I wasn't supposed to feel like I had to bear the weight of world, as a teenager caring nightly for his crying mother after her husband decided to pack his bags and never bring them back home. It wasn't supposed to be the case that I felt like I needed to hide my pornography addiction for a decade and seasons of depression, because I didn't want to be one more source of what was going wrong in our crumbling family. I wish I could say those experiences didn't impact me or my view of God. But that's just not true because I will tell you, it's taken me so many painful years to relearn the truth that I can unload all the heavy burdens I've carried on my shoulders to my good heavenly Father.

Given the pitiful state of broken families in society, I recognize my story is one of millions, and so many more endure far worse hands dealt to them. Yet, even on the opposite end of the spectrum, where a home appears to be all rosy, I promise you that's not entirely true either. Broken people become broken parents who are doing the best they can. For such a reason, no matter the home situation we grew up in, we each need to be reminded that the fruit of the Spirit, which God calls us to cultivate in our character, is also his attributes as a good heavenly Father (Gal. 5:22–23).

So even when our experiences may project otherwise, I pray we each come to embrace our heavenly Father as:

Loving

Joyful

Peaceful

Patient

Kind

Good

Faithful

Gentle

Self-Controlled

Over a lifetime of picking up disappointments, failures, and making poor choices, we can come to carry some heavy burdens and deep wounds that we take into every sphere of life. And we can let others feel the sharp weight of them in an instant—especially in the way we respond to stressful situations, disagreements in marriage, late nights with little sleep, and proudly disobedient kids who don't listen to a word we say until we're full-blown yelling at them. If I'm being transparent, sometimes, after a tough day of parenting, I purposefully remember holding each of my kids for the first time after they were born. Those precious moments are a reminder that my fatherhood must mirror how God continues to father me.

When I was holding my son and daughter for the first time, I was so filled with delight in every little move they made. They had done literally nothing in this world but breathe. Yet I was so proud of *who* they were, as my own son and daughter. And that's precisely the feeling I would imagine the good father had as he saw his prodigal son returning home. It didn't matter how much he messed up; the father's joy for his son was based on *who* he was, not what he had done.

So, when I sit down after the kids are in bed, feeling like a complete failure of a father, I remind myself of the joy I felt in looking down at Noah and Maddie for the first time. And this is exactly how God looks at me in my best and worst moments. Though I may sometimes struggle to accept it as the truth, it's truly the way my heavenly Father feels about me. He demonstrates it in the way that he's slow to anger, kind, gentle, and still proud of me. And that's true for each of our lives.

That's why we desperately need to learn to abide in, trust, and be loved by our heavenly Father. We need to understand what it means to be able to call upon him as our good Father who will take the *first* step in meeting us in our mess. Through trusting in Christ's work on the cross, God views us as one of his own children who can run to him when we're scared, nervous, or just want to sit at his feet. As we're reminded in Matthew 7:9–10, we should run to our Father with all our needs, trusting he will respond with our best in mind. God isn't a malicious father who gives us a snake or stone when we ask for bread. He is a generous Father who wants to meet us in our every need.

If you're a dad, you know the way your son or daughter looks up to you as their hero. You feel the excitement they're filled with as they keep tugging on your arm to wake up early on a Saturday morning to play. Or maybe you can still remember how you used to look up to your dad when you were young and wanted to be just like him when you grew up. This is the kind of heart toward God that he is asking us to have in our lives for him.

As our good Father, he loves us in a way no other can offer, and he wants nothing more than for us to grow into his character and image. The journey of becoming the man of God that we're called to be begins with a reminder of our true sonship in God, because all else springs forth from such grounding. But as we will learn, it's not because of us—our will, strength, or effort—that leads us to become a good and godly man. Instead, as we discussed here, it has already begun by first learning to call God our "Abba Father" and continues by learning to surrender our entire lives to him. That's how God does a good work in us, transforming our old selves into something new and much greater (Rom. 6:6; Eph. 4:22–24).

The Calling of Every Man—a Short Description

As sons in God's family, our primary calling is to embrace him, to be Spirit-led in putting on his character, and to embody his ways of life for those around us. It's to seek and love wisdom from *above*, just as Jesus spoke in his teachings, modeled in his ministry, and mirrored with his life. It's to wake up, ready to fight against every bit of our sin that holds us captive and follow the path of our crucified King—learning to sacrifice ourselves for the gain of others. We aren't called to rescue this sinking ship of a world but to bear witness in it for a mighty God who can mend back together the most shattered of lives. And one day, he will do the same for this world by bringing forth a wholly new heavens and earth, but how and when that happens is his decision, not ours.

Our calling is to help others reject the wisdom of this world and to make God known above all things. We humble ourselves before the one true God to make his name great. It's not about us but about God, who has always taken the *first* steps to rescue and restore us. And now that we once again know him as our good heavenly Father through Jesus, we can respond to our true God-given calling to reflect who he is on earth as in heaven—for the sake of leading our homes, friends, and community for God's greater glory.

Throughout the remaining chapters of part 2, we'll dive into specific focal points of our lives and consider how to surrender them so that we can become the man God has called us to be. From Jesus's calling us to walk the narrow path of discipleship, we must invest our time in practices which cultivate spiritual leadership and wisdom in our lives. In doing so, we learn to walk with God, as well as others on the same journey—in our pain, hypocrisy, isolation, and through the storms of life we may encounter.

Reflection and Group Discussion Questions

1. How would you define your relationship with your earthly father? What positive and negative characteristics of the way he fathered shaped you as a man?

2. How did understanding the parable of the prodigal son from the lens of the father change your perspective on its meaning?

3. When was a time in your life that you felt God took the *first* step to care for you? How has that experience led you to greater trust in him as your heavenly Father?

4. In what ways has your experience, for better or worse, of your earthly father been projected onto your heavenly Father?

5. As you come to understand your heavenly Father more, how has your experience and knowledge from Scripture challenged your assumptions about the way you relate to or come to God?

6

The Narrow Path

"To follow Jesus means that we can't separate what Jesus is saying from what Jesus is doing and the way that he is doing it. To follow Jesus is as much, or maybe even more, about feet as it is about ears and eyes."[1]

Eugene H. Peterson

When we surrender to God, every aspect of who we are is destined for transformed. That doesn't mean the journey will be easy—in fact, it's the opposite. There is a cost that comes with following Jesus. This was true from the start of his ministry—as John the Baptist, who prepared the way for him, was beheaded by Herod Antipas for standing for what was right in the eyes of God (Matt. 3:3; John 14:1–12). The first apostles were asked to drop everything, leave their families, and follow him (Matt. 4:18–22). After the birth of the early church, the apostle James was killed by Herod Agrippa, who also later captured his brother, Peter (Acts 12:1–3). So we shouldn't be surprised that Jesus never spoke of a life in pursuit of God that didn't require our sacrifice. Rather, the right question is, When will it come, and how great will the cost be?

During World War II, Dietrich Bonhoeffer, a German pastor and theologian, felt the full weight of his sacrificial calling to follow Jesus. As Hitler took ground in his European conquest, he also sought greater control of what could be preached within Germany. Dietrich decided to roll up his sleeves and get his hands in the action by joining the resistance, even taking part in a plan to assassinate Hitler.[2] However, like John the Baptist's unwillingness to bow to falsehood, Bonhoeffer met the same fate as he was sentenced to death, most likely by Hitler himself, for speaking out against his evil works and participating in a coup against him.[3]

Bonhoeffer lived by conviction, attempting to maintain as little separation between his beliefs and his actions as possible.[4] During the rise of the Nazi regime, Bonhoeffer released the now-renowned work *The Cost of Discipleship*, whereby he contends that faith in Christ will always require great sacrifice because that's precisely what God has done for us by sending his Son to die. Bonhoeffer suggests that far too many churches have succumbed to a version of Christianity that's faded into secularism and is more defined by a kind of cheap grace than costly grace.

In parallel with far too many contemporary churches, cheap grace downplays the significance of our wayward longings, accountability before God, bringing ourselves to the cross, and the calling to imitate and grow into Christlikeness. As Bonhoeffer pointedly describes, "Cheap grace is the preaching of forgiveness without requiring repentance, baptism without church discipline, Communion without confession, absolution without personal confession. Cheap grace is grace without discipleship, grace without the cross, grace without Jesus Christ, living and incarnate."[5]

An acceptance of cheap grace within the walls of the church results in shallow faith, which far more closely mirrors that of moralistic therapeutic deism than Christianity itself. It's not a bid to "come and die" but to be happy and accept ourselves as we are.

On the other hand, costly grace is the personal invitation to meet the realities of both those words—*costly*, in that it came at the price of the Son of God's life, and *grace* because it gives a man his true life.[6] Bonhoeffer characterizes our calling to yearn for and encounter costly grace in this way: "Costly grace is the treasure hidden in the field; for the sake of it a man will go and sell all that he has. It is the pearl of great price to buy which the merchant will sell all his goods. It is the kingly rule of Christ, for whose sake a man will pluck out the eye which causes him to stumble; it is the call of Jesus Christ at which the disciple leaves his nets and follows him."[7]

Costly grace compels us to surrender ourselves at the foot of the cross, bow before God's throne—condemned in our sin, yet justified through Christ—and say to God, "All that I am is yours."

The sacrifices required to follow Jesus are not merely our Sunday mornings, a once-a-week men's group, or even the perceived fun of a sinful lifestyle. It's the relinquishing of control to define what we believe is best for our lives. It's about putting on the character of Christ and being shaped by the habits and practices Jesus calls us toward in partnership with the Holy Spirit. But as we've already recognized, the call of discipleship, the journey of growing into the image of Jesus as his disciple, is not for the faint of heart nor for those desiring to drift with the all-consuming tide of the world but for those willing to stand against such forces and push forward on a narrow path that leads to true life in God.

A Few Parables for a Disciple's Calling

In the Sermon on the Mount, Jesus goes up on a mountain, sits down, and begins to teach his disciples and followers what will be the greatest sermon on the ways of the kingdom of God (Matt. 5:1–7:29). Throughout his teaching, Jesus lays out the ethical vision of a life wholly surrendered to God, the virtues we are called to cultivate, and the moral commands to which we must hold fast. He invites us to enter the kingdom and walk in his footsteps to become a source of salt and light in this dark world. But as Jesus turns toward the conclusion of his sermon, he offers his audience some imagery to depict the reality of following him.

Jesus summons us to consider a parable on the two paths we can take in life: One path is found through a small gate leading to a narrow and challenging road ahead. The other path has a wide gate and broad road and offers little to no resistance for its travelers (Matt. 7:13–14). Few are willing to find the narrow path, as it requires one to take heart and endure its challenging route. However, like the horde they are, the masses veer themselves through the wide gate, believing this comfortable journey ends well. Although the narrow path promises future hardship, it cultivates a flourishing life with God within its travelers, while the other ensures a slow death disguised in safety. One path leads its travelers to salvation, while the other guarantees the end of weeping and gnashing of teeth (Matt. 8:12).

And then, to bring his sermon to a close, Jesus leaves his listeners with a final parable to tie all his teachings together. He says that anyone who hears his words and does them is like a wise man who built his house on the rock, while anyone who listens and does not act on his words is like foolish men who built their homes on sand. The wise man builds his life on Jesus. When we consider these two parables together, they make the same point from two different angles—Jesus is the gate to the narrow path, and one does not enter the road to the kingdom without entrusting his life to him (John 10:9). And one can only become a wise man by listening to and practicing what Jesus has taught.

Both Jesus's parables complement James's illustration and point of the calling to walk in the ways of wisdom from *above* and *below* (see James 3:13–17). A house built upon the *rock*, walking the *narrow* path, and the ways of wisdom from *above* are all depictions to help us embrace and experience the calling and work of discipleship for our lives. Three different imageries, each describing a foundational element for how we are to walk with, depend upon, and abide with God in this world.

No matter what illustration we choose—following Jesus isn't something that can be half-heartedly undertaken. It requires us to keep our eyes set on him. As Bonhoeffer discusses the narrow path of discipleship, he reminds us of this very truth: "But if we behold Jesus Christ going on before, step by step, we shall not go astray. But if we worry about the dangers that beset us, if we gaze at the road instead of at Him who goes before, we are already straying from the path. For He is Himself the way, the narrow way and the strait gate. He, and He alone, is our journey's end."[8]

Each of our journeys ahead rests on learning to abide in God. Jesus alone is our Good Shepherd, and he has already illuminated this path of discipleship that we walk. He has already put markers on the trail for us to follow and told us how to build a foundation on him as we learn to trust the heart of his Father (Matt. 7:21).

Further, Jesus's sending of the Holy Spirit is crucial to walking the narrow path, so we can participate in the rest of God's story on earth (John 15:26). In fact, the Holy Spirit takes up residence in us to empower our spiritual life (Rom. 8:9). He has come to comfort, encourage, guide, and help us conform to Jesus's image (John 14:26). As J. I. Packer wonderfully puts it, the Holy Spirit's role is to be a "floodlight ministry" that points to Jesus, always directing our attention to Christ, saying, "Look at *him*, see *his* glory, hear *his* words, run to *him*."[9] Through the power of the Holy Spirit, Jesus performed miracles and was raised from the dead. And now the Spirit has come to do the same in our lives, to take what was once dead and broken in sin and make it anew in God (Rom. 8:11).

The Spirit is at work within us—exposing our sins and pruning us of wayward and sinful behavior. But he doesn't just work in our hearts to stop our destructive habits. He dwells within us to help cultivate godly ambitions, desires, and habits so that we become more like Jesus. He's reordering our loves, priorities, and values toward Christ. He's the reason for our transformation, our laying down of sin for the sake of holiness. The Spirit is always with us, bringing us closer to redemption each day, reminding us we are now in God's family, and leading us home to be embraced by our good Father.

And so we must begin each day by inviting the Spirit to continue this work within us—as we walk on the *narrow* path, learning wisdom from *above*, and building our house on the *rock*. Whichever parable or picture you prefer to guide you. The vital component is this: We are men who have chosen to meet the challenging call to be formed into Christlikeness. And though we acknowledge, on this side of eternity, we will always wrestle with fleshly, wayward desires, it doesn't mean they control or define us, as image bearers of God. We've accepted our God-given identity and responsibility placed upon us in the garden of Eden—to represent his reign and rule in every square inch of this world for his glory.[10]

So let us learn the ways of Christ, his way from *above*, and do so well. We have a long path to cover. Where shall we begin in covering the waymakers of this narrow path of discipleship? Or, as Bonhoeffer would have said, How should we learn the practices associated with the costly grace that's been paid for us? Let's begin with a few core practices through an individual lens. In the remaining chapters, we'll dive into further individual and group practices that we must take up on this path.

The Practices of a Wise Godly Man

The aim of these practices is to meet God amidst our time and learn to rest in his presence. Nothing more, nothing less. If we treat these practices as a mere box to be checked as part of our productivity routine, we'll miss moments of growth at every turn. These practices are meant to help us draw near to

Christ because who you spend time with will shape who you become. In *Knowing Christ Today*, Dallas Willard reminds us that grasping a "fact" from a *distance* doesn't actually amount to knowing *it*.[11] We must move beyond knowledge by *description* to knowledge by *acquaintance*, which actually involves getting to know someone or something through personal experience.[12] And the same must be true for our walk with God.

We can say that God is good, gentle, and kind, but if we've not met him intimately in that way, that's a mere abstract conception in our mind *about* God. Such thoughts aren't truths that speak to the character of the God we personally *know*. Nor can we become more like Jesus without spending time with him. For far too many Western churches, this is exactly the route of discipleship that takes place in both the rows and table settings of our church programs. So, as we work through these practices, the focus will be greater on how we *approach* God in them than merely making sure we *do* the activity. Spiritual transformation doesn't happen by mindlessly going through the motions of these practices but by meeting Jesus in them and allowing the Spirit to transform our entire self—our heart and mind—toward Christ (Rom. 12:1–2).

Prayer

Prayer is an intentional time of communicating with God, talking with him as our heavenly Father. We come to him the same way Jesus told us—in private, to discuss our needs and surrender them to our good Father (Matt. 6:6). During prayer, our heart posture with our Father is not transactional, "If you do X, I swear I'll do Y in return," nor to necessarily feel better about ourselves or a situation we find ourselves in. Instead, prayer is more akin to being in an ongoing conversation with God, where he continues to lead us to still waters to sit, be loved, and process with him as he reminds us of who he is (Pss. 23; 145:18). Whether we are seeking protection during life's storms or enjoying a peaceful season of rest, prayer is a time to sit still with God, talk about what's in our hearts, and learn to listen to his voice in the silence (Ps. 46:10; John 10:27).

I recognize it can be challenging to find a quiet space to start our day in silent prayer. My kids wake up at 5:45 a.m., and I know how the other young dads reading may already be lamenting this section. But even waking up twenty minutes before the kids is worthwhile. Or maybe schedule this quiet time at some point in the later morning. Rhythm is so important with prayer. All we must do is simply make the time to just sit with God.

Simply begin by resting in silence for a few minutes before talking with him about how we desire to surrender our day to him. Then just wait in the silence, contemplating who our Father is, what his Son has done for us on the cross, and his continued goodness and faithfulness in our life. Wait in silence, listening for his voice and what true wisdom he brings to our thoughts. He will remind us of who he is and the way he shepherds.

This type of conversation doesn't just have to be in the quiet of the mornings; it can be integrated throughout our day. The apostle Paul tells us we should continue in unceasing prayer throughout the day, finding little moments to rejoice and telling God how grateful we are for him (1 Thess. 5:17). We can have a running conversation with God no matter where we are during the day. We can do so by working through the Lord's Prayer, which reminds us to first offer thanksgiving and praise to God and then surrender our concerns, needs, and temptations to him (Matt. 6:9–13).

Confession

During conversational prayer with God, ask him to search the most hidden depths of your soul—what you are hiding and even that which you haven't discerned—so that you can surrender it to him. If you haven't memorized Psalm 19, I'd encourage you to do so. Throughout this psalm are reminders to ask God to illuminate your mind in how you can come to him in confession, repentance, and asking for refinement. It begins by praising God for all the ways his glory is on display (vv. 1–6), how God's Word refines your character and wisdom (vv. 7–9), and lastly, the call to reorient your heart to desire God's wisdom and righteousness so you can be pleasing to the Lord (vv. 10–14).[13] After reading through Psalm 19, sit with

God and contemplate these different facets and themes with him.

Am I praising God for all the wonderful things he has done?

Am I slowing myself down to recognize his beauty/goodness in everyday moments?

Am I trusting that his law is right and trustworthy?

Am I willfully breaking any of his commands or teachings?

Am I desiring/fearing his wisdom and righteousness in my life?

Am I joyful for the work he's doing in and through me?

Are there any unintentional/undiscerned sins in my life?

Am I holding back from trusting God with anything?

Study

Our study of God's Word is the primary way we come to meet him. If we want to grow in reflection of Christ, we must know his words and let them dwell richly in our souls (Matt. 4:4; Col. 3:16). The Word of God is not a dead book of past events; it's alive and active and used by God to teach, correct, and train us in the ways of righteousness (Heb. 4:12; 2 Tim. 3:16). As Timothy Ward explains, "To encounter the words of Scripture is to encounter God in action."[14] When we come to Scripture, the Father presents himself as the one true God who keeps his promises. The Son—the Word of God—makes him known through his words and works, and the Spirit ministers and illuminates these words for us so we may best understand them and come to know and trust in God himself.[15] The spiritual discipline of being in God's Word cannot be overstated.

In its pages is the origin story of humanity, the reason we find ourselves in the condition we do, the history of God's people, and how he will make all things right again in due time. However, as Willard contended earlier, there is a mighty temptation for studying God's Word to become one of *distant* facts. That's not to say we shouldn't be doing in-depth inductive Bible studies; we should be doing them to sharpen and grow our knowledge of the Word. We should memorize Scripture in order to retrieve it upon any need that arises.

However, we must balance a head knowledge approach with equal commitment to heart transformation. So yes, absolutely grab your favorite study Bible, follow the arguments, investigate the syntax, and learn the proper process of hermeneutics, or interpretation, of Scripture. But we also need to challenge ourselves with a reading practice like *Lectio Divina*, which helps us better hear from, reflect upon, and respond to Scripture in a different way.[16] *Lectio Divina* is a deliberately slow-paced, reflective reading of the Word that dates back to the first-century church fathers.[17] Such a practice also wonderfully prepares our hearts for better inductive study and passage memorization. I encourage you to practice this a few times a week. Go to the appendix and start this practice with Psalm 23. You won't regret it.

Simplicity

The rat race comes for us all—calling us to bow to it the minute we feel we *need* something to be included, respected, or valued by others. Often without recognizing it, we've built our own hamster wheels of temporary needs to feel validated by others. I've been there, and I bet you have too. But we must jump off it before it takes more than we bargained for. Think of Proverbs 11:28, which says the man who trusts in his riches will wither. Our Savior lived simply, and so should we. As Matthew 6:33 reminds us, we must prioritize Christ's kingdom, not build our own. So, how do we best combat this attitude, even sin, of continuing to acquire material goods for their own sake? A life driven by simplicity and being content in God.

Richard Foster describes the importance of simplicity: "It is the only thing that sufficiently reorients our lives so that possessions can be genuinely enjoyed without destroying us."[18] A life committed to simplicity is about cultivating a posture of contentment before God so that we don't need to attach our value and worth to our outward circumstances. Simplicity is taking our wives out for a picnic, watching the sunset, and letting our conversation be the focal point—not expensive food or a unique experience to keep up with our friends. It's showing our kids that we can still have fun, laugh, and play by building forts with cardboard boxes—not depending on another shiny new toy or game console.

And to be clear, it's not that we can't have nice things—but the feeling like we *must* have *those* things to be happy and secure in ourselves. And I promise, if we get caught in this, so will our wives and kids. We must strive to embrace and demonstrate a posture of contentment in God because it will radiate and be imitated throughout the rest of the house. Ultimately, there is so much to gain by opting out of the rat race mentality and realizing that our true joy and needs can be better fulfilled in a slower rhythm of life, which centrally revolves around God, not our busyness. In a world filled with endless desires for more—new phones, cars, trips, etc.—let's show godly wisdom by surrendering to the simple life.

Silence and Retreat

As Jesus withdrew and retreated to the hills to be with the Father, so should we. It doesn't have to be some breathtaking mountain getaway, desert oasis, or beautiful countryside. We just need to learn to be alone (with God). The purpose of silence and retreat is to pull ourselves away from the busyness, confusion, and mundane tasks of everyday life to recenter our minds and hearts on things from above. Most likely, we can't do this practice weekly, maybe not even monthly—but start with planning a quarterly time of silence and retreat, even if it's just half a day out in the local state park.

The goal is to find a secluded place to drop our guard and simply rest with God. Just take a Bible, a journal, and a pen, and put the phone on silent after your family knows you got to your destination safely. You don't need a search crew coming for you! Start by worshipping God. Don't worry, there's no need to sing out loud. Worship is far more about declaring your surrender to him, so start by praying and inviting God to help you make a list of all the burdens you're currently carrying and need to place upon him. Take as long as needed; it may take a few hours.

Then, enter an extended time of prayer where you go one by one through that list, offering it to God and discussing how you are trusting and releasing it to him. Close your prayer time by talking about all the ways he has been faithful in the past and thanking him for what he will do in the future. By the end of this prayer time, you will likely be physically tired—so rest. Sit down, lie down, whatever you prefer—and close your eyes to take in the sounds of God's creation. He takes care of them, and he will take care of you. Enjoy the time, and make sure to get back home on time because, of course, this will be the day the kids are complete rebels, destroying the house, and your wife will need a break.

The Beginning of a Long Journey Ahead

These are just a few of the practices we must learn on the path to becoming like Jesus. But here's the thing: Practices aren't enough. We also have to examine and surrender our mindset and motivations to God. Because, truth is, we can do all the right things for the wrong reasons. Just like Israel wandering in the desert, we must offer God our hearts and ambitions, not just our words and works.

Reflection and Group Discussion Questions

1. When it comes to *cheap* versus *costly* grace, which version of grace most defines your current walk with God? Why do you say that?

2. There's a cost to following Jesus. There's a challenge that certainly comes our way with being on the path of discipleship. How has this been true of your life? What costs have you already experienced?

3. Which spiritual practices are you currently integrating into your life? How much commitment/value would you say you place on them? Are there any practices you need to start? Who can hold you accountable to do them?

4. Consider this: How much different would your life look if you exercised each of these spiritual practices regularly? How much greater would your relationship and intimacy with God be if you did?

5. What's currently holding you back from that kind of life and closeness with God?

7

Becoming What You Worship

"Man's nature, so to speak, is a perpetual factory of idols."[1]
John Calvin

In our fast-paced, instant-gratification, on-demand culture, we can quickly become dismayed by the slow, steady pace required to walk the narrow path of discipleship. In *A Long Obedience in the Same Direction*, Eugene Peterson proposes that we should grow comfortable with two biblical designations as people called to resist the tide of the world: *disciple* and *pilgrim*.[2] As *disciples*, we are called to spend our entire lives devoted to apprenticing under our master, Jesus—learning the craft and skills like novices in the woodshop of master craftsmen.[3] As *pilgrims*, we are wanderers in this world who must keep our eyes set on Jesus in our longing to be home in our Father's house.[4] On many levels, these designations help us hold fast to the realities of what we will encounter as we pursue God and his purpose for our lives in this world.

Behind each of these designations are layers of difficulty we will surely encounter as followers of Jesus. Learning to become more like him and less of ourselves will require an ever-growing level of grace, patience, and trust in God. Just as the early disciples recognized, it will take everything we have to learn the great depths of skill and wisdom to grow in his reflection. We may even stumble along the path—giving into impulsive decisions, diverting our eyes off Jesus, and settling for far less worthy living from the way from *below*. There will be seasons of disappointment, times when our patience grows thin, and we may even question our commitment to God and his best for our lives.

However, that deep longing for eternity will always bring us back to our knees in repentance before God. But, as our good Father, he will be there to meet us. Like the Israelites wandering in the wilderness, we have so much to learn, so much of our old ways to put off, and so great of a journey ahead in walking with God to understand our true purpose and mission on earth. Too often, we assume we know what God is asking of us, while not realizing our assumptions should have been questioned along the way.

A Wilderness Season and a Golden Calf

In the book of Exodus, we find the Israelites enslaved in Egypt, where God will rescue them. Through Moses (and a plight of ten plagues), God confronts Pharoah, who releases his people after losing his son (Exod. 5–13). The Israelites flee from Egypt, but on their way Pharoah changes his mind and seeks vengeance upon them (Exod. 14:5–9). Though the Israelites appear to be cornered, the Lord parted the Red Sea, providing an escape route to the wilderness across the shore, and Pharoah and his armies were swallowed up by the sea (vv. 10–31). But soon after their rescuing, the Israelites began grumbling, complaining to Moses, and doubting whether the Lord would, indeed, take care of them (5:22–18:27).

After the Israelites settle at Mount Sanai, the Lord calls Moses up to the mountaintop, where he offers Israel to be his covenant partner—God's treasured possession, a kingdom of priests, and a holy nation. Moses comes down to share, and the people of Israel gratefully accept (19:1–8). As a result of their commitment, the people of Israel witnessed the presence of God come to the mountaintop, descending like fire in the middle of thick clouds filled with lightning and thunder, causing trembling all the way down the mountain (vv. 6–20). Moses would continue to be called up to the mountaintop so he could relay to the people of Israel warnings or instructions on how they should act regarding their covenant with God.

However, during one of his trips to the mountaintop, Moses stayed longer than expected. The Lord gave Moses the stone tablets inscribed with the Ten Commandments and shared much more about what Moses was to do (24:12). God desired to dwell with his people again, like in the garden of Eden. So Moses received instructions for how the Israelites were to build the tabernacle, where God could reside with them, as well as the ark of the covenant and their altar (25–31). However, rebellion and idolatry were stirring down below.

After forty days on the mountaintop, Moses returned to find the people of Israel had already acted unfaithfully to the Lord—making an idol of a golden calf and an alter for it (24:18; 32:4–5). In the absence of a swift return from Moses (their chosen mediator with God), the Israelites grew worrisome and panicked. In thinking they may have lost their mediator to God, they forged a pagan idol—a calf, which was a common idol image in the Near East that they probably knew from Egypt—as an attempt to *represent* God and worship him. Moses was furious, even breaking the stone tablets God had made. He threw the idol in the fire, put its ashes in water, and then made them drink it (32:20). Though the Lord punished those who made it, he remained committed to Israel. His own faithfulness was enough, even as the people of Israel demonstrated the shallowest depths of commitment.

However, one of the most fascinating aspects of this story is that God's presence was frequently described throughout

Israel's time at Mount Sanai. They shuttered in his presence, which is precisely why Moses was chosen as their mediator with God. So certainly, as Moses was on the mountaintop for forty days, so was the presence of the Lord—the clouds, the lightning, thunder, the terrifying booms and cracks, and, of course, fire! So, why did they not just look up and trust that if the presence of God was still there, so, too, was Moses? As modern readers, it's difficult to reconcile why they would act this impulsively—until we take a step back and realize that even though they were fools, they are just like us.

Their forging of a pagan idol in God's presence is exactly what we continue to do today. You and I can be just as guilty. You see, these wandering, formerly enslaved Israelites saw the greatness of God at work in their rescue from Egypt, but so have we in how God rescued us from our slavery to sin. Israel experienced God's goodness and his provision by giving them all they needed on their journey in the wilderness, and so have we in the ways he meets us in our prayers, and the unexpected ways he takes care of us and our families. Yet, they were frustrated and impatient with how their situation was playing out and how they expected God to work, so they took matters into their own hands to remedy the problem. We have all been guilty of this.

But here's where I want to challenge you, my friend. Many of us think "our golden calf" is the willful sin we continue to fall to, stay addicted to, or hide from others. However, that's a mistaken way to interpret and apply the Israelites' motivation for crafting this pagan idol. The Israelites crafted this idol to represent the faithful God who brought them out of Egypt. Hence, the golden calf is far more analogous to the false beliefs and projections we each hold about who we think God is and what he's asking of us, including how we are to come to him. The golden calf is a beautiful example of how we can quickly adopt and attach our cultural representations, expectations, and purpose onto God.[5] It happens far too naturally in a broken world filled with broken people.

Yet there's another aspect to this tragic thinking: Our false projections about God typically extend much further than we realize. They interweave themselves deeply into how we understand and shape our lives, including how we interpret our role and purpose within this world as men. The reality is even when God is right before us, declaring who he is in his Word and telling us what his greatest commandment is for our lives, we can still build a life and a sense of purpose that's detached from the God of Scripture, who he is and what he asks of us.

Neither Your Sacrifice nor Your Gifts Will Do

As G. K. Beale contends, we will become what we worship (for better or worse).[6] If we hold a distorted image of God, we'll also live out a false image of who he's called us to be. We must understand the gravity of holding onto our false beliefs and attaching them to God because we can grow into the image of a false god, created by our own hands, guided by our false beliefs and self-deception, all in the name of Jesus. Like the Israelites making their pagan idol to represent and communicate with God, we can twist and manipulate God's purpose for our lives. We can contrive our own purpose in life, ask God to bless it, and then pursue it like it's God's best when in truth it has nothing to do with his great commandment and Great Commission for our lives.

The world will attempt to make us believe that our primary calling and purpose in life are anything other than what God is asking of us. It also doesn't help that we now live in a time when our highest calling and purpose are seen as equivalent to our professional vocation when they aren't. In *The Toxic War on Masculinity*, Nancy Pearcey notes the monumental cultural shift during the Industrial Revolution that saw men led out of their homes into the factories and offices of the commercial world. As a result, there was a forfeiting of the biblical ideal of manhood as an engaged husband and father for a narrower, one-dimensional idea of manhood as a mere provider.[7] Another consequence of the father's absence was that wives began taking on the role of being the household source of spiritual and moral formation, whereas traditionally, the man's duty was to lead his family in daily worship—reading Scripture, praying together, and learning the catechisms.[8]

Though this may sound daunting, it is far closer to God's calling of us as men in Scripture. Let me explain by covering the great commandment and the Great Commission in Scripture, as they are interdependent and help us connect to God's direct command and calling for us. When the Pharisees question Jesus about which of the commandments is greatest, he says, "'Love the Lord your God with all your heart and with all your soul and with all your mind.' This is the first and greatest commandment. And the second is like it: 'Love your neighbor as yourself.' All the Law and the Prophets hang on these two commandments" (Matt. 22:36–40).

Our highest calling each day is to surrender ourselves to Jesus. It's to love God with everything we are—in every deep longing, desire, and thought. It's to surrender ourselves to God in complete obedience.

The first commandment is a lifelong calling to seek after the heart of God. It's a reminder of the importance of our vertical relationship with God. Because even if we succeed in every way but get this wrong, we've missed the mark of what God is asking of us. We are mistaken to think our primary calling is to work hard in our careers, be successful, and then offer him a fraction of the spoils as a tithe. This is a grave mistake that far too many men make in the present day. As Hosea 6:6 reminds us, God doesn't desire our sacrifices or our offerings, if we haven't first sought his love. It doesn't matter if we offer God the most precious gifts or sacrifices from our toil if our life remains steeped in disobedience and rebellion.

Each morning, our highest calling remains unchanged—to seek after and love God above all things because this is the fundamental basis of a flourishing life. That's truly where the *good life* is cultivated. Everything hinges on this command and calling from God.

Wisdom from *above* influences every area of our lives, beginning with our relationship with God. Our vertical relationship with God determines the quality of our horizontal relationships with others. One pours out into the other. That's why Jesus follows the great commandment with the calling to love our neighbor as ourselves. But we're often confused by Jesus's statement that we should love our neighbors as ourselves. Should I love them like the selfish, fallen, sinful person that I am?

Absolutely not. Remember, that's not who we really are! We are God's image bearers, bestowed with inherent dignity and respect and worthy of a calling to follow in the footsteps of Jesus. Just as we were never too far gone or beyond the reach of God's grace, neither are our family members, coworkers, and random strangers we walk by each day. We treat our neighbors as ourselves because, in the eyes of God, they are worthy of being treated as we have been, and the grace that we have received from him ought to be poured back out to those around us. That's how the grace of God works in and through us.

Our ability to love others, particularly those difficult to love, is a litmus test of our spiritual maturity. Accepting our daily calling to love God will make us more like him. Slowly, day by day, greater mirroring him than our old self. It all comes full circle—the greater we recognize the love of God bestowed upon us, the greater we realize the responsibility to pour it out to those around us.

Hence, before Jesus returns to heaven, he leaves the disciples (and us) with the Great Commission to make disciples of all nations, baptizing them and teaching them to obey all that he has commanded (Matt. 28:16–20). When we ask what God's will is for our lives or his calling for us, we don't need to treat it as a mystery to be discovered. It's to learn the depths of God's heart so we can help others experience God's love and mercy in the same way. It's as simple as that:

Love God.
Love Others.
Make disciples who do the same.

No matter our professional vocation, our first and highest calling is to love God and others as we partner with God to fulfill the Great Commission to make disciples that reflect his goodness and stand for his truth in this world. I'm not saying our jobs that put food on the table aren't important;

it's just that the way we earn an income is not our primary source of identity or our main calling. Our God-given calling is to use our passions and gifts to share the gospel and make disciples—whether we're paid for it or not. And that calling isn't something we tap into just when we're on a mission trip but every day in our homes as a husband, father, and friend.

The Starting Place of a Disciple Maker

When we discuss the Great Commission, I recognize there's an assumption that it's a task to be done on a foreign mission trip, most likely in a Third-World country. However, that instinct is far more a product of the Western mindset of expansion and globalization within the American church. So I'll be rather blunt about this because it's too important—the starting place of our calling to be a disciple maker is not in a distant land but within our home. As husbands and fathers, God has called us to be the spiritual leader of our homes—the ones who instill true wisdom from *above*, serve with a humble heart, and mirror God's own love to each member of our family and anyone else who walks through our door.

Our homes are the starting place of disciple making because that's God's proper design and order for the family. God has placed upon us, as men, an incredible role and responsibility to lead our homes spiritually. Just as we are called to lead the church body, so, too, are we called to lead our families. However, *how* we lead is just as crucial as recognizing our call to leadership. We are not to adopt or pursue our own model but a servant-hearted leadership style that directly reflects how God continues to father us and aligns with the words and ministry of Jesus.

We have a clear depiction of the leader we are to become. As we recognize *how* Christ loved, served, and offered himself for the church, we, too, are to lead our homes in a holy and blameless manner (Eph. 5:25–27). In colonial times, the home was ordered in reflection of society's structure. Fathers were seen as the priests of the home, teaching on moral and spiritual matters, discussing the story of God and his people, practicing the spiritual disciplines with his family, caring for the needs of each member, and serving them in love.[9] Our day job that provides a roof over our head and shoes on our kids' feet is a wonderful blessing. But make no mistake, we each have a far more important calling—and our effectiveness in being a good, godly husband and father depends on everything we have discussed in prior chapters.

In an age of fatherlessness and loneliness, our homes can become a refuge for those needing care, rest, and wisdom. Whether it's the neighbor's kid down the street whose parents are divorced or an adult friend going through a rough season, our homes are the front lines for making disciples. When our children become old enough to witness their dad's friends coming over for men's group to sit around the fire, to laugh and encourage one another, to open the Word and pray together, they will notice (believe me). And so, too, will they notice our intimate walk with God and the ways he is transforming our lives, shaping our hearts to love the same things he loves, and ordering our priorities as they ought to be.

We are the leaders of our homes. Who we are and what we do matters. If we choose to drink from the well of wisdom from *above*, those around us will naturally follow in our footsteps. That's not a promise, but it is a proverb (Prov. 22:6; Deut. 6:6–7). If we run to our Father in all seasons of life, they will see that in our walk. When we stumble and fall, when we have a rough day as a dad (as we all do) and confess it to God and ask for our wife or kids' forgiveness, they will start to cultivate the same heart. The most courageous decision we can make as a man, husband, and father is to own our brokenness before our loved ones and take them by the hand to meet the Good Shepherd together.

We don't need to be a perfect father or follower of Jesus—that's impossible. However, we do need to pursue obedience ruthlessly. Even our everyday mistakes can be opportunities to reveal how God is at work within us. If we genuinely believe Psalm 23, then we can trust that our Good Shepherd will take us (and our family) to still waters, providing rest for our souls and guidance on the narrow path, which leads to an abundant life in him.

Our family and friends will follow our lead and imitate us. Even if you're single or married without kids, this is true for you and anyone who enters your home. Our character and posture are naturally being adopted by the onlooking eyes of those who look up to us. Remember, what we worship is what we will become. The path we walk is also the one we're inviting others to follow.

So may we each take up the great call to seek him, identifying and rejecting our false assumptions about who the Lord is. May we grow in how we connect with God and how we run to him for who he really is. When we pursue him, it sets us (and our families) on a trajectory to experience the depths of his character. Learning the fullness of his great commandment is precisely what stirs our hearts to love and disciple others as Jesus would. It's the grounding for what cultivates us to become godly leaders. What we most deeply desire and long for in life is also what we will grow into and reflect.

So, as we close this chapter, I'll leave you with this: As we each come around the table to eat this week, may we each be the leader God has called us to be. Bring your wife, kids, and friends along with you on the journey of the narrow path. Lead them in prayer and tell them what the Lord is teaching you in your quiet time with him. If you've messed up, tell them about your disappointment in that decision. Offer them a challenge and truth about life, and tell them how wisdom from *above* can guide us through life's trials and rough seasons. We set the tone and culture of our homes, so surrender that space to God and immerse it in the truth and wisdom of the Lord. That's our highest calling. We lead by example—by serving their needs, putting ourselves last, and making disciples of Jesus within our homes—because at our core, we are striving to be God-fearing husbands, fathers, and friends.

Reflection and Group Discussion Questions

1. What false beliefs/projections about God, or the ways you are to come to him, might you still be holding onto? Are any of your false projections about God related to how your earthly father has acted toward you?

2. Before reading this chapter, what would you have said is your main calling and purpose in life? How does the calling of being a disciple maker not dismiss your professional vocation but place it in its proper place of importance?

3. How would you assess your home as a place of discipleship? Where do you need to grow as the spiritual leader of your family?

4. Share a story of a time when you have modeled your faith to your family and they naturally just noticed. What were you doing? Were you able to use it as a moment of instruction or teaching with your family?

5. Everything about our walk with God shapes how we lead our families and our treatment of others. How does this understanding continue to shape your priorities to make time for him every day?

8

The Weight of Burdens

"We never have to pretend with God, and genuine brokenness pleases God more than pretend spirituality."[1]
John Ortberg

The world offers a great deal to help us stumble or entirely fall off the narrow path. And at every turn, the enemy also conveniently places temptations that entice us to wander over to his well of wisdom from *below* and drink it in. However, if we're transparent with ourselves, many times, we don't even need the aid of the devil or the world to ruin our lives. We just have to be foolish enough to listen to our own sinful desires and act on them. We can fall in so many different ways. It's the sad but honest truth. To make matters worse, after moments of slipups and bad decisions, it's far more common for us, as men, to run and hide in our embarrassment and shame than to run to him in vulnerability and weakness.

For many men in the West, the consequences of isolation and loneliness have bubbled to the surface in the ugliest way. It's become a silent epidemic that has led so many men into the grips of sin. Given our cultural conditions and the broader setting of our modern technology, it can be far too easy to slip in and out of the shadows of sin without anyone noticing. For each of us who have struggled with a hidden addiction, we know this feeling intimately. It's a place of emptiness that can be so numbing that it becomes a disturbing yet soothing source of comfort.

Maybe you, too, have felt such a hollow feeling of hopelessness, all while clinging so tightly to it for safety. For some misguided reason, we stay there, holding onto the false security of darkness and isolation. Even though it's such an incredibly lonely place that overflows with sadness and despair, time and time again, we opt to remain isolated in our deepest pain. However, this choice to embrace our loneliness only further produces a darker, vicious cycle of toxicity within us, multiplying the weight of our burdens far more than we ever imagined it could. And they can be so heavy, pressing down on our shoulders, that they hold us back from experiencing any joy that we once knew, let alone the peace we once felt in walking closely with God.

Whether it's the consumption of pornography, a drinking habit that has taken deeper roots than we want to acknowledge, a gluttonous way of life, or one of the other many unhealthy coping mechanisms we can select, we must learn to practice handing over our burdens to God. Because the truth is, we can break free from the sin and shame cycles that imprison us. We can choose to embrace the trustworthy words of God to slow down, rest, and take refuge in him. He is a good Father willing to meet us at our worst. But we must be willing to show him our deepest pain, hypocrisy, and sin.

It's no small task to learn the practice of transparently coming to God with who we really are, but it yields a freedom that is so rewarding. Along this journey of transparency with the Lord, we also recognize that the church is a hospital for the hurt, lonely, and weary coincides with Jesus's willingness to carry our burdens. Jesus doesn't expect perfection in our lives, but he does call us to come to God with our brokenness, for he is the only One who can mend us back together. Even if we have doubts when we read these words, we are not beyond God's hand of restoration and renewal. He's been in this business for thousands of years.

The Burdens of an Unexamined Life

Many men seek help far too late. As a pastor, I sit across the table from men who know every bit of this cycle of loneliness, pain, and shame. Sometimes they reach out because they've hit rock bottom and have no one else to help put things back together. It's unfortunate, but most of the time, they're also newly separated or divorced after their spouse learned of their sin that was done in the shadows. These conversations are always tough because they hit home for me.

I always leave these meetings wondering what could have gone differently. What could have changed, or what steps could have been taken so this wasn't another story of a collapsing family? The reality is that nothing about the inflicted pain that's unfolding in that home will remain isolated to just this man or his wife. It'll fall on each household member, no matter their age.

Little do these men understand that, as a teenager, I was on the receiving end of this kind of pain. For far too many of my friends who grew up in Orange County, California, where there's a revolting 58.8 percent divorce rate, this is just a regular part of life.[2] Of course, I'm not advocating that the normalcy of divorce doesn't negate the sharp wounding of such. Believe me, it doesn't. You don't have to be a sociologist to recognize our current decaying culture and connect it to the breakdown of the American family. There's an emptiness, loneliness, and waywardness that we've not previously seen in our nation's history, and it impacts every facet of our spiritual condition.

However, the most challenging part for me now is that I constantly hear the same overarching theme throughout my conversations. I could offer a real-life example with a pseudonym name to help immerse us in these conversations, but the reality is: I don't need to. Many of us have lived this story and experienced this exact conversation after a friend (or you) asks to grab a meal and proceeds to describe the following life situation.

For many years, he put his nose down to the grind and now wholly recognizes that he ignored the devastating growth of sin in his most private desires and thoughts. Though, looking back, he felt he needed to keep pressing on. There were bills to pay, vacations to take, and pricey purchases to keep up with the neighbors. Work also became an idol, and excuses were at the ready—projects that had to be done *now* and couldn't wait until Monday. On weekends, the only option was to divide and conquer, with one kid playing a sport here and another on the other side of town. He withdrew his presence as a husband and a father. There was no time to check in and catch up after a long week. As a couple, they had lost their connection and physical touch within their marriage.

However, more excuses come forth: "We're just in a busy season." But the growing truth is that he didn't care for or desire to protect his marriage. Neither did he take time to care for himself or the vices that slowly took deep root in his life. And so, in all this busyness, one day, he made a detrimental decision that revealed all the accruing cost of wisdom from *below* that he'd been drinking for years. Now, pick your poison in relation to the situation—maybe it was having an affair, taking comfort in booze and being arrested for a DUI on the way home, or being caught hiding a porn addiction. That list of examples could be far greater and grows by the year. But whatever the nature of the fall, there's always a significant catalyst moment when his wife decides to kick him out and serve him with divorce papers.

When I ask something to the tune of, "But why did you not seek help or say something sooner to a friend or me?" He replies along the lines of, "Because, even if I knew exactly what was so broken in my life, I probably would have just seen it as a *tension to manage*, not a *problem to deal with*." And here's the thing: He's probably right. Far too many of us are running toward burnout because we have adopted the cultural lifestyle of an unexamined and unsustainably hurried pace of life, not just for ourselves but for our families as well.

The Quiet Life of a Disciple

The unexamined life has consequences. It's not a question of *if* things will come full circle in our lives but *when*. And the only men who don't take stock of such a statement are the same ones who are attempting to outrun it. But more than that, for those who claim to follow Jesus, busyness (over long periods) absolutely counters the healthy spiritual formation God desires for our lives. As Paul reminds us in his letter to the Thessalonians, we should aim our ambitions toward living a quiet life for God so that our daily life wins the respect of outsiders (1 Thess. 4:11–12). In direct contrast to the rushed pace of this world, we should learn the tempo of a slow, quiet pace of life, which remolds our hearts and minds toward peace, self-examination, and gratitude to God.

In *The Ruthless Elimination of Hurry* John Mark Comer suggests that love and hurry are often incompatible.[3] Even more pointedly, he contends that the great enemy of having a thriving spiritual life is, in fact, our own busyness.[4] I couldn't agree more. When our fuel gauge runs low (or empty), the unintended consequence is a lack of prioritization to examine, clean, and care for our soul. So please hear me when I write this: Busyness will eventually bury you, whether physically, mentally, or spiritually. In fact, our lack of willingness to slow down will slowly but subtly grow to be the enemy's greatest way of deceiving and distracting us from God's will for our lives.

The devil wants nothing more than to overwhelm our schedules and cause turmoil in our daily rhythms. Because, if we're always on the run, we won't have time to slow down and be *with* God.[5] We won't have a moment to take in the forest from the trees and ask ourselves, "*Is this the life I truly wanted?*" And here's where we return to Paul's words to the Thessalonians: If our life reflects the rat race of every other father in the neighborhood, it's rather difficult for others to notice God working in and through us. When our ambitions align with the chaotic pace of this world, our daily rhythms and values will reflect such, whether we come to acknowledge it or not.

The sly strategy of the devil in the rat-race lifestyle is filling our minds with the idea that it just costs time and money. In reality, it yields itself to be a perfect opportunity for him to start seeding unhealthy and sinful desires from *below* much deeper into our hearts. And when those deeply planted toxic seeds grow into roots, it's simply a matter of time before they influence our character and actions, producing more significant burdens upon our souls.

I know you think this won't ever be your story. Let me share some wisdom from the other side of the table—that's what they all thought too. I'm telling you, the lack of concern for your family's hurried rat-race pace of life can be the starting place for what leads you to sitting across from a friend or pastor, with your hands over your face, saying, "I feel so stupid. I can't believe it's come to this." More often than not, these words are genuinely spoken from a now embarrassed but convicted heart. But nothing about the authenticity of their words changes the situation they now find themselves in nor the fact that the enemy knew it was always possible for them to arrive at this dreadful place.

Our increasing loyalty to busyness—whether for our work, dreams of success, or family commitments—is just one way we ignore the sin and strongholds we are building up in our lives. It's become the central excuse for many men feeling stuck in a dry, empty spiritual place. Otherwise, I wouldn't have woven it into our discussion. But truthfully, it's just one mistaken way among many, including an overreliance on human willpower, that we put on blinders and set up roadblocks to real-life transformation. It leads to forfeiting what God really wants for us—an honest and vulnerable relationship—for something far less—a shallow, consumer-driven relationship, which dishonors God and his best for our lives.

Weakness Is the Way

God doesn't want us to pretend with him; we don't need to. He already knows our best and worst character qualities, our most proud and embarrassing moments, each step forward we take in growth, and the vices that hold us back. Yet, ironically, we still try to act like there remains a little tucked-away part of ourselves that he can't see. Again, it's rather humorous because he's already aware of our most private thoughts and actions done in secret. God is all-knowing—even seeing through the actions to the heart of *why* we're doing it (Ps. 139:1–4; 1 John 3:20). So here's my encouragement to let go of our fear in coming to God at our worst and with our heaviest burdens, because he's already there with us, brothers.

God's never been surprised by the ways we can make complete messes of our lives. He knows them all too well because Jesus, himself, was willing to sit and eat with the lost and lowly. When the Pharisees questioned Jesus about why he would spend time with the despised tax collectors and sinners, he said, "It is not the healthy who need a doctor, but the sick. I have not come to call the righteous, but sinners" (Mark 2:17). Christ came for those who don't have everything figured out, so why do we later come to God and walk through the doors of his church *pretending* that we do? Is it because we don't really trust that he loves us and will offer us grace and mercy?

Put this into perspective: If Jesus regularly broke bread with sinners during his ministry, why should we be afraid to come to him at our worst when we're offering our entire lives to him? For those in pain, suffering, caught in the traps of addiction, or struggling with anxiety about the hardships and unknowns of life, he is there with open arms, ready to be a source of refuge. Instead of being weighed down in burden and lost in the world's ways, Jesus says to cast all our burdens on him—he can take it (Matt. 11:28–30; 1 Pet. 5:7). But we have to be willing to share our burdens with him. He will not force us against our will to do anything, even when it's best for us.

We must consciously surrender our heavy burdens to God in prayer, where the real work begins. Giving God the difficult matters in life is what grows us into strong, godly men. I recognize it's been culturally drilled in us for generations as men, but we don't have to be strong enough to hold everything together. Rather, we must be courageous enough to accept that we can't fix every situation or ourselves. When the enemy tells us that it all falls on us, it ought to be a trigger to remind us what a liar the devil is (John 8:44). Instead of lying to ourselves that we are strong enough to withstand the weight of our burdens, God calls us to walk in weakness. His church is a hospital for the hurt, lonely, and afflicted, drawing us to meet him in our weaknesses.

Paul's words cut straight to the heart on this matter, when he writes to the Corinthians, "Therefore I will boast all the more gladly about my weaknesses, so that Christ's power may rest on me. That is why, for Christ's sake, I delight in weaknesses, in insults, in hardships, in persecutions, in difficulties. For when I am weak, then I am strong" (2 Cor. 12:9–11).

If we want to grow into maturity, to be good godly men, we must transparently meet God in our weaknesses. Remember, these words come from the same man who also said, "For what I want to do I do not do, but what I hate I do" (Rom. 7:15). We all have a sinful flesh, which is why we will need to fight against it until the day we die (v. 18). Nothing about learning to surrender our burdens and sins is for a temporary seasonal fix. It's a lifelong practice, so that we may grow into the man God has called us to be.

For those stuck in the vicious cycle of shame and addiction, you won't win that war by simply running away from it. You must pursue something better—peace and freedom in God—by being in his Word and mediating on its truths.

However, that goes for every man, as we learn to surrender our fleshly sinful desires over to God in transparency. And for those that carry heavy burdens, whether a physical illness or a difficult life circumstance, you can trust God and hand it over to him.

Brothers, we aren't strong enough to bear any of these kinds of burdens. Rather, we must invite the Spirit to cultivate a heart of surrender within us. As we walk alongside God, we can choose to hand everything over to him. And we should because we were never meant to endure those burdens alone. Our inherent limitedness as humans is a gift from God that signals our great need of him. This is the nature of God's upside-down kingdom, where our weakness is a vessel which propels us toward true godliness, strength, and wisdom.

As we learn to hand over our burdens to God, his power is at work within and through us. We are like clay jars, who illuminate his light (2 Cor. 4:7). The more we surrender our burdens and trust him to hold us together, the greater his light shines through us for all to see.

To close out this chapter, I'd like to recommend a few spiritual disciplines that help us surrender ourselves and burdens to God. The first is fasting, whether physically or digitally. Fasting is an incredible way to focus on God, asking him for guidance and even help in knowing what we should be surrendering to him. I would encourage each of us to turn to the appendix for the prayer of confession and self-examination.

Try to do this practice out loud. There is something powerful, even healing, about speaking openly with God. As we will discuss in our next chapter, sharing with other trusted men in deep community is also pivotal for our spiritual growth.

Reflection and Group Discussion Questions

1. How do fear, isolation, and loneliness impact your life? In those moments, is your instinct to run toward God or away from him?

2. We each carry burdens, sin, and shame in our life, the question is, What are you doing with your burdens? Are you honest with God about who you are?

3. Have you practiced confessing your sins out loud to God? Take the next five to ten minutes and do that now. If you are in a group setting, during your discussion time, share how you felt during this experience with them.

4. Why is it essential to regularly contemplate that Jesus sat and ate with sinners? What does this mean for your life as a sinner and how you see and treat others around you?

5. Is there an area of your life more defined by pretending than being honest about your weaknesses with God? What is the cost of holding onto your hypocrisy?

9

Don't Go Alone

"Everyone says they want community and friendship. But mention accountability and commitment to people, and they run the other way."[1]
Tim Keller

In the aftermath of World War I, C. S. Lewis and J. R. R. Tolkien wrote literature that captured the true nature of our world and the heart of man—in all its tragic mixture of courage, heroism, suffering, and wretchedness.[2] Both witnessed the depravity of the front lines—the barbed wire that tore flesh, constant gunfire, the sound of the flamethrowers, the desperation to find their gas masks in time, and the everyday smell of death.[3] Their lives were never the same, and neither was their community of close friends, as both lost nearly every close friend in the war.[4] However, soon after they arrived at Oxford University, they bonded over their mutual admiration of Icelandic mythology.[5] It was the start of a friendship that would change the landscape of literature and impact millions of readers by leading them to consider God's truth, beauty, and goodness in a devastatingly painful world.

However, when they first began to get to know each other in 1926, they were in different places with the Christian faith. Tolkien carried his Catholic faith to the front lines, while Lewis struggled to understand the central tenets of the faith and remained an unpersuaded skeptic.[6] Yet, on September 19, 1931, the hands of fate would bring together Lewis, Tolkien, and Hugo Dyson, a friend and lecturer at Reading University, for a conversation that would radically change Lewis's life.[7] After staying up until four a.m. discussing the nature of myths, Lewis began to wrestle with whether the story of Christ was the true myth, which really occurred in history.[8] Twelve days later he would write to a friend that he now believed in Christ.[9] That conversation was his turning point.

For the next two decades, these men, along with a few others, would gather at The Eagle and Child Pub as a small group of Christian writers, known as "the Inklings," to discuss their faith, writings, and life. In the context of these friendships, Lewis's faith grew deep roots, and he and Tolkien crafted a multitude of critically successful works, including The Lord of the Rings and The Chronicles of Narnia. But more significant than any monetary success or critical praise for their work was the acknowledgment of the true value of friendship. Lewis would write, "Is any pleasure on earth as great as a circle of

Christian friends by a good fire?"[10] I would agree; only a few other moments can compare to that sense of joy.

We each deeply long for authentic, meaningful friendship—a group of men who will stick by us in the best and worst seasons of life, celebrate our victories, and sit in silence with us in our losses. We each desire to be in our version of "the Inklings." As Lewis suggested, there's something special in sitting around a fire deep into the night, where conversation goes from serious matters to uncontrolled laughter. Those nights can be refreshing to the soul. And the truth is, we need those nights more than we often say. That's because we each desire a group of men we can trust to walk through life with us, laughing along the way and reminding us to take in the forest from the trees.

The antidote to our contemporary epidemic of loneliness is deep, transformative life-giving friendships. As we discussed in our last chapter about coming to Christ in weakness and vulnerability, we should also learn this practice with *trusted* friends. But before taking that step, we must first examine whether we have the right guys in our corner. I'm not advocating every friendship needs to reach that depth of intimacy. Certain friendships should remain at shallower depths, whether that's due to trustworthiness or several other reasons. Yet I hope your men's group can become a place of deep trusted community, where each man is fully known, seen, and heard for *who* he is and *where* he is in his walk with the Lord.

Finding the Company We Ought to Keep

Each of us recognizes we need a group of men around us that has our back, speaks the truth to us when we need it, and holds us accountable. But that won't happen if they don't see it the same way. The friends we allow to speak into our lives, challenge us, and steer our formation must share the same foundation in God that we hold for our lives. So, as we think about who is in our inner circle of friends, begin by asking/praying about these questions:

Is Christ at the center of their life?

A question of faith and loyalty.

Do their actions, character, and vision for life align with God's calling?

A question of obedience and wisdom.

Are they willing to have difficult, uncomfortable, and vulnerable conversations?

A question of care and vulnerability.

Are they desiring the same kind of friendship?

A question of mutual agreement and commitment.

For Christian men, deep community and friendships share one core trait: a commitment to build our lives on God's calling. Too often, we assume we must share the same hobbies, passions, or life stages to be close friends. If you're in that place, I understand your perspective. However, I would encourage each of us to take a different approach. Deep friendships are cultivated through encouragement, discussions on how each is yearning to grow in Jesus, and offering the vulnerability to support one another on that path. Good friendships come about by learning the depths of another's story, soul, and longings and venturing together on the difficult, narrow road.

This is one reason the best men's groups are typically made up of guys from different walks of life—who don't act, look, or necessarily have all the same degrees or experiences. When the group is too homogenous, unhealthy comfort and temptation can settle in, often leading to a repeated routine of shallow talk. Unfortunately, these conversations typically take precedence over the more important, deeper matters of the heart. A diverse group of guys must work to make connections, cultivating a skill in which we, as men, tend not to be specialists—the art of active listening. It requires more up-front commitment and investment, but long term, their bonds are usually stronger because each person's uniqueness is an opportunity to learn something outside one's own gifting and life experience.

However, when analyzing how deep community and friendships are cultivated, I've found a more fundamental dynamic at work that we must recognize. The longer I've worked with men, the more I've noticed it's not on us, our willpower, to manufacture deep community. Instead, the Holy Spirit orchestrates and cultivates it. C. S. Lewis suggests the same notion, describing that God brings together our inner circle of friends to teach us the meaning of friendship, like an instrument, which reveals the beauty of being known by others.[11] Lewis's words are dead-on. It's fascinating to ponder how we've met our closest friends and how God's hands were involved. Many times, God helps us stumble into the right friendships just as we need them. He ordained us to cross paths at the right time and place and discover we each are walking in the same direction, looking for the same thing.

But perhaps you don't have this kind of community. Unfortunately, many don't. I don't want this to be a chapter you quickly dismiss. Many men who reach out to me do so to find deeper community, looking for a place to belong and be known. I recognize that even for some reading this chapter, it may feel off-putting or be another reminder of the wounds of loneliness. Please don't let that temporary feeling dictate future seasons of life. On the other hand, another set of readers may be contemplating decades-long friendships, realizing that those relationships aren't as life-giving or fulfilling of the framework of genuine Christian brotherhood that we desire. Either way, there is a place where it can be found.

The heart of deep, vulnerable community and friendship is cultivated when we express our desperate need for God with others. Men's groups should be designed with that purpose in mind. We don't even need to know one another prior to entering the group. Let God steadily cultivate that work. This is precisely why our local churches ought to be the first place we seek to find community and friendships. When we consider the criteria for the kind of men who should be the company we keep, our churches are filled with men matching that criterion. Our local churches are in a prime position to strike the loneliness epidemic. We just need to open our doors, invite them in, train them, and send them back out into the chaos of this world to face their battles together.

The Call of Friendship—to Mordor and Back

I won't hide my cards when it comes to my all-time favorite works of literature. Tolkien's The Lord of the Rings is the most profound, convicting, and accurate depiction of the reality of our world that's been offered in fiction. In fact, Tolkien noted that the trilogy was meant to communicate his Christian worldview and society's moral descent, which would lead to greater chaos.[12] In many ways, it's a brilliant work of applied theology, illuminating the true nature of friendship, evil, temptation, sub-creation, suffering, and God's providence.

From the trilogy's beginning to its end, Tolkien draws us in to recognize the biblical portrait of friendship between Frodo and Sam. We are first introduced to them in the peaceful Shire, where the call to friendship appears lighthearted, even on the worst days. However, circumstances quickly change. For most of the story, we follow Frodo, the ring bearer, and Sam along their quest to Mordor to destroy the great Ring of Power. If you've read the tale, you know it's a path marked by a dark, sorrowful reflection rooted in Tolkien's experiences from the front lines. Unbeknown to us, along their journey, we discover that the real hero of the story is Frodo's best friend, Sam, who faithfully walks with him as they encounter new challenges, dangers, and evils that lurk behind every corner.

On multiple occasions Sam saves the day. His most heroic scene comes toward the end of the story, as they near the entrance of Mount Doom to destroy the ring. At the pinnacle of their journey, Frodo collapses from exhaustion, attempting to crawl forward with the bit of strength he has left. In Frodo's most desperate hour of need, Sam musters all his strength and courage, picking him up over his shoulder to carry him closer to the entrance of the Mountain of Fire. And during this moment of bravery, Sam cries out, "'I can't carry it for you, but I can carry you and it as well. So up you get!'"[13] When we understand the context, it becomes an even greater picture of the true call and duty of friendship we should strive to have with one another, as brothers in Christ.

Sam was not called to take up the ring himself; such a toilsome burden was reserved for Frodo. So, what does Sam do? He carries his best friend and the immensely heavy burden wrapped on a chain around his neck. You must understand that every hand that holds the ring seeks to possess it, slowly take control, and ultimately lead them to be wholly consumed by the dark powers of evil.[14] Tolkien described this powerful ring as a weapon, representing the true nature of evil and sin, which summons us to become our own foolish, twisted god.[15]

Whether Tolkien meant to or not—although I'm sure he did—he crafted a beautiful portrait of our calling to bear one another's burdens. As believers, we don't have to let such a weapon (sin) rule our lives. First, we have the Holy Spirit to illuminate our walk with God. But second, deep friendships are another means God designed for us to off-load our burdens. We need close friends who know the sin we hold in our lives and who will step in to help us shoulder the weight as we look to unload it. Just as Sam could not carry the ring, we are not called to bear the responsibility of our brother's sin (Gal. 5:6). Yet true biblical friendship calls for us to pick up our brother off the floor of sin and shame, which eagerly waits to devour his life.

The Freedom and Joy of Being Known

As men who desire to pursue God above all else, our deepest and closest friendships should be aligned and characterized by these two key verses: Galatians 6:2, the calling to carry one another's burdens, and Proverbs 27:17, the calling to sharpen one another in mutual accountability and dependency on Jesus. If we're serious about growing into the wise, faithful men God has called us to be, we must find the right community to support us. Because the simple truth is, we can't do this alone. The path of true wisdom from *above* and salvation is not one that can be walked alone but alongside other *trusted* men on the same journey.

We all need a community of trusted friends who recognize and speak truth into our blind spots and pick us up when they see us falling. When the powers of darkness feel close to our homes, godly friends are the first to combat it in prayer. When we have had a difficult week, where nothing has gone right, and we take it out on our wife and kids, they step in to encourage and remind us to model confession and ask for forgiveness. As Acts 2:42 describes, we cultivate true biblical community by balancing his call upon our lives to surrender to him—devoting ourselves to the Word, fellowshipping by breaking bread, and praying together. That's how we do *real* life together, as men.

As every member of an addiction recovery group learns, there is relief and power in confessing out loud *who* we *really* are. As fallen men, we will constantly grapple with a sinful flesh. So we must put down our guards and stop pretending that we don't wield weapons of sin every day aimed at ourselves in hypocrisy and self-destruction. We each walk through seasons of pain, self-inflicted or not, and we need to be seen, heard, and known. If you have never participated in a men's spiritual formation retreat that spurs these kinds of discussions, try the retreat plan in the appendix with a group of men from your church. It's too important to neglect this aspect of your Christian journey. We must walk through the trenches together, holding one another up, because there's no other way to fight the good fight (1 Tim. 6:12).

It will cost time and comfort, but true freedom follows being known by God and a few *trusted* friends. Our good heavenly Father and our close friends want his best for our lives and our families. As we close this chapter, I pray that one day you will know the joy of walking through years of different seasons with a close, trusted group of friends. One day you'll step back in prayer and praise God for all he has done in and through them. No matter whether you're walking through the most perilous of times, facing the future in fear and trembling, or enjoying the sweetest of seasons:

Don't go alone.

Reflection and Group Discussion Questions

1. What are the main qualities you look for in a friend? How would you currently describe the community you surround yourself with?

2. Most men struggle to find friends today. Has this been true of your story? How did you intentionally seek out community and friendship?

3. If you have a group of close friends, how did you meet? Do you now see God's hand in the way your friendship developed?

4. What keeps you from being vulnerable with other trusted men? Fear of rejection? A sense of loneliness that you'll be the only one with a particular struggle?

5. How has this chapter challenged or grown your understanding of the call and duty of Christian friendship and brotherhood?

10

Unshaken

"Suffering, then, is the true badge of discipleship. The disciple is not above his master."[1]
Dietrich Bonhoeffer

At the close of the Sermon on the Mount, Jesus says that anyone who hears his words and follows them is a wise man who constructed his house on the rock. Anyone who half-heartedly listens, ignoring to put them into practice, is like a foolish man who built his home on sand. As we covered in chapter 6, "The Narrow Path," the call of the wise man is to build his life on Jesus and his work on the cross. However, in our prior discussion, I intentionally skipped over an element of Jesus's parable so that we can dig into further detail here—the fact that Jesus says the storms of life will come equally for the homes of the wise and foolish (Matt. 7:24–27).

We will all face tribulation and suffering in this world (John 16:33). I don't say that as a proverb; it's just the human condition. Neither the wise nor the foolish man can avoid the suffering that comes to test his life and the strength and durability of his home. The original listeners of this parable would have immediately grasped the importance of Jesus's claims about the devastating nature of the storms that could sweep through their towns. The land surrounding Israel is known for heavy rains, and its desert valleys can quickly become impacted, rapidly producing a flood zone—making these moments the true quality test of one's home.[2]

It wasn't until a heavy storm came rolling through that they realized whether their foundation *actually* stood on solid rock or shifting sand. On a beautifully clear and sunny day, no one believes their home is built on shaky ground, soon to collapse. But here's the thing—as it was true for their homes, so it is for ours.

Of course, Jesus's original listeners would have taken this parable more literally than we do about the physical danger of storms. Yet it still rings true for our lives. We'd be remiss of Jesus's point if we thought he was merely speaking in physical terms. Instead, his use of storms in the parable is also meant to apply metaphorically to the trials, tribulations, and suffering life frequently brings. Hence, a storm of life is any source of suffering we encounter. As Jesus's parable calls us to recognize, these storms have a way of revealing what lies in the deepest parts of our hearts, the foundation of our lives.

We can't always predict when the storms of life will arrive, but they will come. We live in a time and place where there's always an oncoming storm on the horizon and another possible one coming at us from the other direction. So, as men, we must learn to walk with God amid our suffering, recognize our emotions, and practice vulnerability as we come before him. We need it for ourselves, but our families also need to witness this side of us, too. Because it's where trust is built in our homes and how our children realize they can run toward us, not hiding in their own sin and suffering.

Come Hell or High Water

Life can be cold and callous. We can be hit by so many different types of storms of life that we never saw coming—a cancer diagnosis, betrayal from a loved one, job loss, or suicide of a friend. My wife, Kristen, and I walked through a few tense seasons of back-to-back storms, even when we were dating. Just in a short period of two years during college, she lost her brother to leukemia, her house burned down, and I struggled with an eight-month bout of illness/depression that left me bedridden by migraines, pain, and anxiety. We were each desperately falling to our knees, asking God, "Why does the rain just keep coming?" I wish the Lord audibly responded to those pleas. I don't think God sent these storms. But either way, those were the first of many storms to test us in life.

All of our households will continue to be tested by the storms of life, just as was true for our parents and their parents and all the generations that came before them. That's just facing the pain of our human condition. Some storms are even self-inflicted via addiction, alcohol, drugs, porn, or any other poison. We're also encountering a newer set of storms that force us to wrestle with and grow in our knowledge of Scripture and our need for wisdom from *above*. These storms often leave us confused and frustrated in how we are to respond to the moral decline of Western culture and have been brought right to our doorsteps. Each of us will face storms in this life; the question is: Have we built our lives on a solid foundation to endure them?

Considering all these storms, Jesus's parable is a sobering reminder for our lives. By the end of Jesus's sermon, we are told his audience had grown into a crowd (Matt. 7:28).[3] They listened intently, were amazed at his teaching, and acted as though his words were important for their lives, which is why Jesus's last parable is so significant to ponder. Even in their clear amazement, he still led them to contemplate what foundation upholds their lives. He wanted them to wrestle with the difference between building a home grounded in true wisdom from *above* and foolishness from *below*.

As the parable describes, our foundation reflects that choice: Did we listen with an attentive heart and follow Jesus's commands or ignore putting his words into practice?

Ultimately, Jesus asks us to consider our final judgment before God. Have we built our lives on his foundation or built our home on something else that was laid in vain? That decision isn't one isolated in time. It reflects where we wish to make our bed for eternity.

There's no other way to say it: The ramifications of this parable are both temporal and eternal. Jesus is painting a picture that the storms of life reveal snapshots of ourselves in real time, which prompt us to consider where we stand with God. As we encounter these different kinds of storms—pick any of the ones I've described—each one has its own way of pulling back our skin to reveal the foundations of our heart and home. Each one challenges us to the core in a unique way—whether physically, emotionally, relationally, or spiritually. That's just their inherent nature. Pain and suffering have a way of bringing us to our knees and revealing *who* we actually are and *who* we trust with our lives.

That's why the storms of life, for better or for worse, can be a source of clarity for our identity. Have we been truly walking *with* God or merely knowing *about* God? Those are two different paths that lead to two different identities and foundations of life: One choice results in growing as a wiser, humble man with greater intimacy *with* God. The suffering produces a heart that desires to listen and obey him in the middle of the chaos. While the other option leads to foolishness, keeping God at a comfortable distance as we hear his Word but remain in the shadows of self-reliance. It can lead to deceiving oneself and others with knowledge *about* God—though never inviting him to transform our lives and the wounds of our heart.

If we're being brutally honest with one another about applying this parable, the latter applies to the faith of cultural Christians. They embrace the goodness of Christian community, while unwilling to remove their mask, drop their guard, and admit their brokenness to God and others amid life's storms. They want to enjoy God's blessed community while not sacrificing their wayward life upon his altar. This is precisely why Jesus's parable was a warning to his original listeners and one we must continue to heed. The storms of life and the suffering that comes along with it always have a way of taking the floor out from beneath us to reveal the foundation we've built our lives (and our families) upon.

We can all pretend that our homes are all cleaned up and organized well, even throw a fresh coat of paint on the walls—yet, when the wind comes howling, the only feature of our home (life) that matters is our foundation. Because of that truth, we, as men, must step up and lead in seasons of both suffering and peace, modeling a faith worth following even in the most violently turbulent storms of life. But here's the catch: We don't do this by acting like we have it all together—rather, the opposite. Regardless of the kind of storms and trials that come rolling into our lives, we are responsible for leading ourselves and our homes by practicing emotional vulnerability *with* God amid it all.

Practicing Vulnerability Through the Storms, Suffering, and Pain of Life

For many of us walking through difficult seasons of life, we often feel like we just have to bite down, grit our teeth, and power through. There's no changing the situation, so we just have to make do and endure it. I get it—I was there for a lot of my life. Frankly, that's what most men are taught. But then, when we step back, doesn't it feel odd that we're supposed to act like real men and be tough—by stuffing down our emotions, pretending we don't have them, suppressing them further down until we become emotionally numb? It's one way we ought to realize how culturally formed our definition of manhood is, even as we talk about "biblical manhood" within the walls of the local church.

We can't hide from the truth. We will face multiple storms throughout our lifetime along with the chaos, grief, and pain that follow them. So, why wouldn't we strive now to cultivate a more biblical approach to the storms in our lives? God doesn't ask us to just keep ignoring or enduring our way through them. We must step forward on the narrow path, walking the steps of those who have gone before us, and learn to abide and rest with God in life's greatest sorrows and frustrations. When our wife and kids witness us vulnerably sitting with the Lord, that's how generations are impacted for the kingdom.

We find such an example in King David's life. He's often cited as an exemplar of the wise man (1 Sam. 18:5, 14, 30) we should strive to be. He's also described as a true man after God's own heart. Even the apostle Paul acknowledged him for this (Acts 13:22; also see 1 Sam. 13:14). David was a courageous man of God—a dangerous one, too. He straight-up killed a giant on the battlefield and confronted all types of conflicts, evils, and injustices. I love all of that about him. We typically do well to discuss David's character in light of his wisdom and faithfulness while also affirming his deep brokenness as a man, which led to some poor decisions.

But, too often, we neglect to discuss the essential feature of what defined David, as a man after God's own heart. Maybe it's because it feels so unmanly, considering his experience and skill on the battlefield. But it wasn't David's heroic moments that God necessarily delighted in. Rather, it was because David would run to him in every storm that passed—in each of the moments of fear, guilt, hurt, loneliness, shame, and joy—and process these emotions of the heart *with* him. That's precisely the nature of the Psalms, as David is crying out in desperate transparency and vulnerability. He isn't just willing to acknowledge the truth of his actions and heart but also how he *feels* on the inside. Whether David felt anxious, forsaken, or overwhelmed with joy in the Lord, he was open *with* God about it (Pss. 3:1; 22:1; 34:1–4; 51:1–6).

As men, we must imitate David's openness with sharing his emotions *with* God. Believe me, we all have them—they're in there. In *The Cry of the Soul*, Dr. Allender and Dr. Longman III describe the importance of recognizing our emotions: "Emotions are the language of the soul. They are the cry that gives the heart a voice. To understand our deepest passions and convictions, we must learn to listen to the cry of the soul."[4]

When we face the suffering and pain of life, our emotions are the essential connection points between our inner and external worlds.[5] Our emotions are like built-in signal markers designed by God to help us process our situation and surroundings.

For some of us, maybe the first challenge of this chapter is to recognize how we feel in a particular moment. If you're not familiar with what Dr. Chip Dodd refers to as the eight primary human feelings, he wonderfully explains and leads us to contemplate each in his work, *The Voice of the Heart*:[6]

Hurt
Lonely
Sad
Anger
Fear
Shame
Guilt
Glad

Next time you're in a situation and you can't wholly discern what you're feeling, turn to this page. Identify the feeling and then seek to understand *why* you feel this way.

Sometimes that answer is easy. Other times we must ask a series of questions to excavate and clarify such: Does this current feeling come from a healthy or unhealthy place? Is it our sinful flesh prompting it, or is the Holy Spirit evoking this emotion, so we can mend a past wound? Am I feeling this strongly because of a past experience? There are many questions we can ask, and we should do that hard work. If emotions communicate the deeper matters of the heart, then we must discern the source that's stirring within us.

It's why, in the raging seas of life, our emotions tend to bring to the surface our most deeply held assumptions and questions about God.[7] Think about when the disciples were at the mercy of the great storm on the lake, fearing for their lives, and they wake Jesus (Matt. 8:23–27). To the surprise of many readers, he rebukes them. It wasn't necessarily because they were terrified—again, that's just human emotion being triggered as we process the dangers of our external world. Instead, Jesus was rebuking their underlying anxious assumption that God would abandon them in the middle of the storm. They let fear and anxiety take control of their decision-making, not their faith. That's what Jesus was rebuking.

Our emotions reveal the deeper condition and desire of our hearts—for better or for worse. When properly recognized, our emotions lead us to greater intimacy and vulnerability with God. Dodd reinforces this point, as he writes, "Vulnerability exposes neediness, and neediness can lead us to seeking and knowing others and God."[8] Our deeply felt emotions are God given and are meant to draw us into a vulnerable conversation with God, where we can openly share and surrender our needs to him. Yet, on the other hand, our emotions are still disordered or mismanaged because of our sinful flesh, which can potentially lead us into further spiritual unhealth. Hence, the importance of Scripture's call that we invite God to transform our inner world—the heart, soul, and mind (Rom. 12:1–2; 2 Cor. 4:16).

Our neediness, our desperation, is an invitation for God to do good work within us. We, as men, must recognize it's okay not to be all right in the middle of the storm. If we're truly a man, we should follow the footsteps of King David, pleading, "Where are you in this, Lord? How do I know it won't always be like this? I'm hurting, my family is hurting; when will we experience your peace?" When life is falling apart, and we're angry about that, we must be secure and vulnerable enough to tell him and cry out in our pain! He can take it.

We don't need more men stuffing their emotions and drinking to numb their pain. We need courageous men who face their own emotions and pain and process them *with* God in the middle of the suffering and storms. We don't need to run away from him but to run toward him in our pain, steeping ourselves in his Word, and meditating on his truth day and night, so that our hearts might be transformed (Ezek. 36:26; Heb. 4:12).

The Lord is our refuge and shelter amid the storms of life (Ps. 46). And under his safety, we also learn to process how we ought to feel during these seasons. David's vulnerability and neediness for God is what made him a man after his own heart. And it's what he continues to expect of us when we're walking with him. David's life was filled with storms that tested his foundation in life. Yet, as he reminds us, we must let these seasons of trials and tribulation be a sobering test of whether we're truly building a sure foundation upon God himself.

We will never be unshaken as men, but our brokenness can drive us toward God in desperate neediness, where we can stand upon an unwavering foundation in Christ alone. Our trust of God in the middle of the storms of life and suffering is the true measure of a man. That's our calling and responsibility through the trials of life, and as we model how to surrender to God, we will impact the next generations within our homes, at our churches, and in our communities. Our vulnerability with God cultivates our emotional maturity, godliness, and wisdom as leaders. It's where we learn to hold onto God, not ourselves.

Reflection and Group Discussion Questions

1. When you look back on your life, what storms have impacted you? How did those past storms impact you as a man? How did they make you feel in the moment?

2. Are there any storms you're currently walking through or recognize coming in the distance? How can you best prepare yourself for those seasons ahead?

3. When you look at the foundation of your life, how would you currently assess it? Are there any faults hiding beneath your floors that would lead to a collapsing foundation?

4. Vulnerability is vital for a thriving relationship with God. How does recognizing your emotions with him fit into your practical everyday life? Is this a growth spot for your relationship with the Lord?

5. How do you need to grow in grasping your neediness of God? Why does it feel like men take this statement negatively, when it is a positive?

6. How does your men's group currently practice vulnerability and discuss your emotions with one another? What can you all do to grow in that practice? What would it look like for you to do this with your wife and kids?

11

Dying to Live

"We know we are surrounded by the untruthful and hypocritical, but our generation has come to accept it as normal and thus to be manipulated by it."[1]
Francis Schaeffer

Year after year, it seems as though our world keeps falling further into the shadows of despair and immorality. As we've peered out at culture, we've seen a creeping darkness looming in the distance. We recognize that it was always out there but not too close to home. Yet it slowly crept forward, shrewdly scaled itself up and encroached its way over into our city walls and onto our front doorsteps. The great moral descent of Western culture has begun, and it's causing an enormous wake that we can no longer ignore. Its consequences are far-reaching and have left many of us questioning how to wisely lead and navigate the situations we find ourselves in.

In *The Rise and Triumph of the Modern Self*, Carl Trueman contends that we live in the age of *deathworks*—a term to signify attacks on established cultural art forms that reflect our deeper underlying moral fabric of society.[2] At the heart of their mission is to make old values appear absurd and foolish.[3] These cultural attacks are meant to subvert and dismantle the sacredness of our society—hence, taking the rainbow (a sign of God's covenant) and reinterpreting it to signify sexual liberation.[4] Another prime example is pornography, which throws out any dignity and intimacy for a lesser, perverse vision of sex with the aim of profit and third-party viewership.[5]

Our culture has pridefully exchanged God's moral order for profane falsehoods in the name of inclusivity and vanity. Augustine's prophetic words continue to ring true: a depraved love of self will be given the highest honor in the City of Man.[6] The disordered, misguided self is celebrated, and the masses now cheer and rally for what should repulse us. We live in a world that has embraced and normalized wisdom from *below*. However, there's no going back to simpler, less morally complex times. Pandora's box has been opened; we can't change that. Yet we also have no reason to feel defeated.

The call of the narrow path shines all the brighter in the darkness. I recognize that's neither convenient nor a consoling truth. But like the many generations of witnesses before us, it's our responsibility to represent the ways of Jesus's kingdom amidst our faltering society. As God's ambassadors, we are called to be light, salt, and a source of true wisdom in this wayward world. But we must ask: How do we meet that call daily? Our answer lies in the words of our Savior, as he sent out the disciples—to take up our cross, follow him, and find our life by losing it. That's the only way forward worth eternally pursuing.

Wolves, Snakes, and Your Allegiance

In Matthew 10, Jesus prepares his disciples to be sent out on their first missionary journey. At the beginning of the discourse, Jesus provides instructions for how the disciples were to carry themselves in each town and reach the lost people of Israel (vv. 1–15). He also tells them they've been given authority and power by God to perform miracles—heal the sick, drive out demons, and even raise the dead. Don't worry—I'm not about to suggest we're supposed to do all that! All those supernatural tasks were reserved for the apostles during that time, yet I'm not entirely sure you'll love what's coming next either.

From verses 16–42, Jesus broadens the scope of conversation to what all his followers will face in the present and the future as they represent him in this world.[7] At this turn, Jesus also shifts into a darker, more apocalyptical tone, describing what awaits us when we proclaim his name. He warns us that we're being sent out as sheep into a vicious world of wolves

(v. 16). To walk wisely in this world, we must learn to be just as shrewd as the snakes, while remaining innocent as doves when we face opposition (v. 17). Jesus readies us for worst-case scenarios, including relying on the Holy Spirit to speak through us, when we are arrested and thrown in front of governors and kings to bear witness about him (vv. 18–20). And to tie it all in a nice apocalyptic bow, he says you will be hated because of me; even your family may turn on you (vv. 21–22).

Jesus isn't setting the stage with this harsh reality out of fear tactics, though. He's forcing us to consider whether we are *actually* willing to commit our allegiance to him if this is what unfolds. A student is not above his teacher, nor a servant above his master. Rather, we share in his footsteps as we walk, and we should expect to share in the same fate (vv. 24–25). His point is rather clear. As followers of Jesus, we should expect suffering—to have our reputation drug through the dirt, to be unfairly treated, to be ridiculed for upholding God's values in a world that tosses them away. So, if we find our culture is filled with debauchery and a negative attitude toward Christianity, we must ask ourselves why we would expect anything different. Jesus never claimed otherwise. In fact, he forewarned us of what we now experience.

But first, place yourself in the headspace of the disciples when they heard this. Remember, they had no reason to believe Jesus would later be crucified. Many still hoped Jesus would build an earthly kingdom to demonstrate his authority and power. In the story arc of Matthew's Gospel, Jesus hasn't even performed some of his most well-known miracles, like the feeding of the five thousand, or hinted at his future death and resurrection, let alone his arrival in Jerusalem. As modern readers, we stand in the privileged position of knowing how the whole story unfolds, making Jesus's following words all the more important.

Jesus reminds them (us) not to be afraid of what will come, even if opposition marches right before us. Our assurance is in the fact that the Lord is greater than any forces of darkness. God is on our side, watching over us, as we step into the darkness of this world to testify about his great name (vv. 26–33). As we walk through the trials and tribulations of this world, if we acknowledge God, he will acknowledge us, but if we disown his name in front of others, he will not claim us later (v. 33). Like Jesus's parable of our homes amid the storms of life, he tells us that how we faithfully stand in opposition reveals our true standing with God. Again, God is not interested in our half-hearted commitment. We are called to offer all our devotion to God, even in the face of rejection from our own families (vv. 35–37).

We're in the middle of a spiritual war. Jesus made that clear. We're either for him or against him (Matt. 12:30). There are only two sides to which we can swear our loyalty. Contra to the hippy peace-loving Jesus many love to portray him as, he outright says he didn't come to offer peace but a sword in the fight against darkness and evil (10:34). As we will discuss in the next section, how the battle against evil would be won (and how we are to carry on the fight) looked so different from what many expected, including the disciples. But we mustn't skip over Jesus's message here. If we have offered our allegiance and loyalty to God, we have to put on a biblical worldview in interpreting the brokenness, conflict, and opposition we face.

Even amidst its remaining beauty, this world will never be our true home, source of comfort, or peace. It's naïve to place any other expectation upon it. A part of being a follower of Jesus is recognizing that for every good we've built, another ten will reveal the despair and evil entrenched in this world. We shouldn't deceive ourselves of the spiritual battle around us. Call it what it is—we live in a world that's still in rebellion against God. And we're called to face this spiritual battle every day of our lives and fight against the evil principalities of this world by listening and imitating Christ himself. That's our battle cry, and we do it for God, ourselves, our family, and our friends.

An Invitation to Truly Live—Pick Up Your Cross and Learn to Die Daily

The world may be falling apart before our eyes. We may be watching the exchange of every truth for a falsehood, but our role as faithful men remains constant through the chaos. Jesus makes no bones about it—we will be a witness amidst the darkness and evil that surrounds us. We are called to courageously step forward in faith. As Jesus brings his conversation of preparing the disciples (and us) to a close, he offers the following challenge: "Whoever does not take up their cross and follow me is not worthy of me. Whoever finds their life will lose it, and whoever loses their life for my sake will find it" (Matt. 10:38–39).

In the first century, to take up one's cross was a bid to come and die in the most miserable of ways—death by crucifixion. Yet that's precisely what Jesus would do for us, as he bore our sin.

Jesus's words are an invitation to put our self—all our self-created identity, hopes, desires, and dreams—to death. It's a summons to join him in the ways of self-denial upon the narrow path of salvation—to reject our wayward desires that stem from *below* and learn to live for God.

If we say we are ready to pick up and carry our cross, it's not a Sunday morning exclusive duty. It's a vow we take to the grave. It's a daily commitment to throw ourselves off our own altar of worship and, instead, kneel before the one true God in vulnerable confession and self-examination. It's to trust our Good Shepherd in a world that holds no promises of keeping the wolves and snakes at bay. It's to wake up each day and hand over our fears, shame, and worry to God. It's to be willing to surrender and suffer for his name's sake as we practice thinking less of ourselves and serving his name in greater ways.

To find true life in Christ, we must cling to the work of the cross. Our spiritual formation into Christ's image will only proceed as far as we are willing to die to our self and live in renewal of who God has called us to be.[8] Our calling to die daily leads us to uplift God and all those around us, replacing our self-satisfaction with serving the needs of others. God did not place our family and friends in our lives for what they can offer us but for what we can offer them. Our love and service for others should match the depths of our comprehension of God's love for us on the cross. I know so many men who claim they're willing to die for their family if they were in harm's way. But how about we just start with learning to serve them the way they need to be served?

I pray that each of us will realize our role as men is to love and care for those around us to the point of death. To lead spiritually comes at a great cost and often appears more as serving than it does resting in authority and power. If we desire to be men after God's heart, then answer the call by leading and serving those in your home, church, and community from the inside out—dropping to our knees to pray with our kids, encouraging and reaching out to loved ones on the worst of days, and most importantly, offering the most precious of gifts—our time and wisdom.

God has entrusted us to serve those around us whether they're a part of our biological family or not. Our churches and communities need good faithful men who recognize this calling. We need good godly men who raise up others in the way from *above* by personally inviting them on the same path. The way we seek to serve and care for those around us is also the measure of trust we earn amidst the wolves and snakes who seek to influence and prey upon them.

As we make one last turn, I would encourage each of us to stop and consider our own future death and legacy. I know it can be a difficult topic to approach mentally, but there's a reason Jesus calls us to ponder the possibility of our death. It matters—those prayerful moments of meditating on our death can spur Spirit-led internal conversations in our minds and hearts about the convictions we hold in the here and now. It forces us to consider the path we're walking, the man we're becoming, the people we love and serve, and the time we have between now and our last breath. Thinking about our death reveals what we hold most dear and to whom our greatest loyalties belong. And for every follower of Jesus, we truly learn to live by surrendering our life.

There's Only Two Kinds of Men—Choose Wisely Who You Become

Let me be open about how I thought about my death and legacy during the writing of this work. I pictured my grown kids burying me. I imagined what they'd share at my funeral. I envisioned them cleaning out my old belongings and laughing about the memories represented in those boxes. And I cried thinking about them holding each other, as they looked at pictures of my wife and me. And for each one they looked at, I saw in their watery eyes how grateful they were that we sought to mend the brokenness we carried by surrendering it to God. And they talked about us as we grew older, grayer, and wiser, that our love wasn't just beautiful but a picture of what Christ has done for each of them. That's the legacy I want to leave my kids, and I hope each of us can share in wanting the same.

Throughout our time together, I hope I have conveyed that I recognize our lives are full of complexities and gray matter. Yet not everything in life can be viewed through this lens. So, as we draw this conversation to a close, I don't want to mislead or excuse away the type of men we are becoming. If our Savior didn't pretend there were more than two sides, I won't either. I beg you to wrestle with this truth prayerfully: there are only two kinds of men—those defined by their surrender to God and cultivation of true wisdom from *above* and those in rebellion of God and their drinking in of poisonous wisdom from *below*.

Jesus has called your name.

Reject yourself and walk upon the narrow path.

Come and die so you may learn to live until your very last breath.

Reflection and Group Discussion Questions

1. Why is it essential for every believer to recognize Christ's call to pick up his cross? What role does the Spirit have in helping us do that on a daily basis?

2. How does your faith call you to love and serve those around you? Provide a few examples of how the cross shapes how you treat others.

3. As you look back through your time in reading this book:

- What chapters or topics impacted you the most? Why do you think that was the case?
- Were there any sections that challenged your walk with God? What steps should you consider taking because of this?
- Overall, what key takeaways will you hold onto? How did your understanding of what it means to be a faithful man grow?

The End of the Beginning

This is just the start of a long journey, my friend. God isn't asking for perfection in our lives as we learn to live for him, but he does require that we fall to our knees in our brokenness. That's why we've begun walking together at this place on the narrow path. It is a spot where many tend to rush past because coming to God with our hidden wounds and assumptions about him can be daunting. Yet it's necessary for an honest relationship with him and our spiritual formation. As we pursue God, we must carry ourselves in reflection of who we really are as we are being made new in Christ. God's doing a good work within us. Let us trust him in that.

Our responsibility is to cling to the cross of Christ each day and openly proclaim our desperate need for his grace and mercy. Rather than trying to coerce a fallen world to change its nature, let us do what God calls us to: surrender to Christ. It has to start with us—that's how it was always meant to be. Take up your cross, reject the call of the world, and desperately seek and cling to the heart of God. He will take care of the rest in due time.

As men, our lives ought to reflect the true cost of discipleship. As we further venture upon the narrow path of life, those around us should notice less of ourselves and more of Jesus—mirroring his trust in the Father and dependency on the Spirit. They should witness our deep yearning to trust God in the messiness of life and see that to do so is sweeter than any honey we could taste and more rewarding than any amount of gold we could hold. As we steep ourselves in his Word, may others around us take notice of how God is radically transforming our entire self—our desires, character, and habits to greater reflect Christ. May we be a witness for his kingdom. That's the rest of the journey that each of us is called to walk together.

I pray that on the way, each of our hearts have grown stronger and our eyes more focused on how God is calling each of us to lead our homes, churches, and community. I'm not one for cliché endings, but this is just the beginning of a long road ahead, brothers. No matter what comes our way, may we each keep holding up the light in a dark world. As his image bearers in a wayward world, may we each cling tightly to the cross, proclaiming our allegiance to the Lord and his kingdom.

Appendix 1

Lectio Divina

Lectio Divina, meaning "sacred reading," is one of the best ways to steep ourselves in Scripture.[1] Find a quiet place where you won't be disturbed. If this practice is unfamiliar, start with a known passage like Psalm 23. This will be such an impactful exercise to work into your spiritual habits and routine.

Step 1. Read (2x)

Start by reading through the passage twice. On the first read through, read the passage out loud slowly. Take time to emphasize each word. On the second reading, continue to read it out loud, but more heavily emphasize the words or phrases that catch your attention.

Step 2. Meditate

Now read the passage a third time. Invite the Spirit to press into why this word, phrase, or truth is connecting with your life right now. Ask yourself: Is this directly related to something I'm walking through? A past wound? Be patient and ask God to connect the dots to help you. By the end of this step, you should be able to better understand why God prompted you to recognize these specific words or themes in the passage.

Step 3. Pray

At this point, come to God and ask him to dwell with you on these matters that have connected with you in the passage. Ask the Lord to help you wrestle though the question, What are you asking of me in light of the truth of Scripture that has been revealed to me today? Close this step with praising God for who he is, as well as for revealing his truths in the Word to you today. If you need to ask for forgiveness or guidance, make sure to do so. Thank him in advance for recognizing your needs, and tell him that you trust him to meet all your needs.

Step 4. Rest and Contemplate

The last step is to rest and be silent with God for a few moments. Give yourself a pause before continuing onto your next task of the day. Remind yourself what God prompted and how his grace and mercy are more than enough.

Appendix 2

Prayer of Confession and Self-Examination

A prayer of confession and self-examination requires admitting our frailties as broken human beings before God. Honesty before God and with ourselves allows us to be open to seeing our blind spots. The instructions for this practice are a combined and modified version of a few confessional practices found in Calhoun's *Spiritual Discipline Handbook*.[1]

Step 1. Read

Begin by reading Psalm 32 slowly and prayerfully. Read the Psalm so that your heart softens to the benefit of surrendering your sin to God, seeking the freedom and openness with him to be gained, and acknowledging the hinderance if admission is withheld.

Step 2. Prayer of Self-Examination

We hold a great deal of hidden sin in our heart. Invite God to search your heart. Ask him to expose any forms of sin you may not be aware of, including any form of lying to him or yourself, envy, jealousy, bitterness, gluttony, lust, or pride.

Step 3. Confession

As God draws you to recognize the sins in your life, write them down. If you have wronged a specific person, write down their name. After you feel like this list is complete, pray over each item, confessing your wrongdoing to God, asking him to forgive you and to show you if any additional steps need to be taken to make things right.

Step 4. Prayer of Gratitude

Close your time by thanking God for his mercy. Praise him for the ways in which he sees you through Christ, not your sin. Praise him for making a new creation out of you.

Appendix 3

Men's "Story" Retreat Guide

Men's retreats ought to have a specific end in mind—whether that's a time of group fellowship, discipleship, or rest and solitude. Men's retreats that are done well typically tend to serve one of these purposes. In my experience, a men's retreat shouldn't be primarily oriented around speakers and sermons (a teacher-driven retreat). They should center on matters of the heart—inviting God and others to know greater depths of participants' story and walk. The goal of retreats should always be to become greater known by God and the other men.

For this reason, I'd recommend the "story" retreat for a men's group that has yet to go on a retreat together. It's specifically meant to help foster vulnerability and trust within a group. You don't have to go to an official retreat center. If it's just your men's group, you can book a cabin or getaway location that can accommodate your group and has an open area where you all can chat.

A few weeks out from the retreat, have each man pen his life story in order to share it on this retreat. The goal is for each man to share for twenty minutes. Now, to help each man share, have each follow this rhythm of storytelling:

1. Start with where you were born and the dynamics in your family of origin. Who was present in the home? Were there any generation patterns of sin, etc.?
2. Jump to a snapshot of your life at fifteen years old. Describe what life was like for you: Did you have many friends? What were your greatest moments of joy, passion, vices, challenges, and disappointments?
3. Give summaries of your life by decade, offering significant moments of excitement, adventure, and failures. Do your best to accurately portray your life stories—not inflating the best moments or leaving out anything embarrassing or shameful. Share your real story, not the one you think they want to hear.
4. Focus greater attention on the moment, or season, of surrendering to Jesus. What preceded that decision? How did your life begin to change in the following seasons after?

5. Close with the present. If someone was watching your life from a distance, what type of man would they see? What are your values and longings in life? Where do you need to grow? What priorities may need to be shifted? What areas of your life would God be pleased and proud of?

Make sure to take at least two full days for this retreat, preferably three. Provide a schedule for when each guy will share his life story. The best way is to group three guys together for a ninety-minute session with five minute breaks between each sharer. That will leave the group plenty of fellowship time or time for some preplanned activities to do together.

The key to this retreat is balancing the times of deep vulnerability with fellowship and laughter. Try to close out all group sharing time before dinner each night so you can make a fire and have some solid time of stories and laughter around the campfire.

If you want to stir up some great conversation, go around the circle asking: How did you meet your wife? What's the worst job you ever had? What is your most embarrassing moment on a date, at work, or in marriage? What is your biggest pet peeve or self-admitted worst quality about yourself? You get the gist of the type of questions that make for a good time.

Before you leave the retreat, plan a final group session to pray for each man. Affirm the men in their willingness to share their stories—the best and worst moments—and how God is working in their lives.

Gratitude

Sometimes less is more, and brevity deepens the weight of the words we write. So, to each person who has poured your time and wisdom into me: *Thank you with all my heart.* You know who you are; no amount of thanking could adequately convey my appreciation.

- This book wouldn't be in your hands without the steadfast faith, patience, and sacrifice of my wife, Kristen. Through every season of chaos, confusion, and peace, our love hasn't withered but grown stronger. You're the best part of me through thick and thin and many late-night edits.
- Noah and Maddie—for all the ways you two continue to help me recognize a true heavenly Father's love. I'm so proud to be your dad; nothing could ever change that.
- Past and current men's ministry leadership teams—I'm indebted to each of you for your encouragement, love, grace, and willingness to speak truth into my life as a

husband, father, pastor, and brother. Your friendships mean the world to me, and your willingness to walk in the trenches of life and ministry together is a blessing beyond measure.

- My literary agent, Erik Wolgemuth, thank you for your encouragement, guidance from the outset, and willingness to take on this first-time author. It's been a true gift to work together.
- Jeff Simmons and Rolling Hills Community Church—so much of what we've walked through together in ministry is at the heart of this book. I couldn't be more grateful for a senior pastor who recognizes the impact and power of building up godly men for the sake of their families and God's kingdom.
- Jason Williams, Rob Jacobs, and Rex Minor—for your care, investment, friendship, and mentorship. I still hold close those years of ministry together and your grace, kindness, and willingness to pour into a young pastor who had (still has) so much to learn.

- Justin Porter—when all was falling apart, you were there. Thanks for being the hands and feet of Jesus and pointing me to the narrow path, instead of self-sabotage and destruction.
- The B&H/Lifeway team—I never imagined this journey together would begin over coffee and some good conversation. Many thanks to Brian Daniel. Logan Pyron—wonderful job with the edits and making my first book process seamless.
- And, of course, God, who has come to my rescue and saved a wretch like me. I still feel unworthy of the call you've placed on my life. Though, in your grace and my anxiety, you are a Good Shepherd who continues to lead me beside still waters to rest. You are with me, and that's all that matters in a wayward world.

Notes

Chapter 1

1. Augustine, *Confessions*, trans. Sarah Ruden (Modern Library, 2017), 3.

2. I combined the ideas of James 3 with Charles Taylor's discussion on the importance of Augustine's language of inwardness and perversity. See Charles Taylor, *Sources of the Self: The Making of the Modern Identity* (Harvard University Press, 1989), 138–39.

3. James K. A. Smith, *Desiring the Kingdom: Worship, Worldview, and Cultural Formation* (Baker Academic, 2009), 24–27, 51. Also, see G. K. Beale, *We Become What We Worship: A Biblical Theology of Idolatry* (IVP Academic, 2008).

Chapter 2

1. C. S. Lewis, *The Abolition of Man* (Harper One, 1944), 26.

2. Cormac McCarthy, *The Road* (Vintage International, 2006).

3. Stephen J. Nichols, *Bonhoeffer on the Christian Life: From the Cross, for the World* (Crossway, 2013), 31–32. To make matters even worse, Adolf Hitler believed he was ushering in a society of those truly in the image of the Lord, as John Kilner describes in his work, *Dignity and Destiny: Humanity in the Image of God* (Eerdmans Publishing Co., 2015), 20–22.

4. For those wondering how this might theologically make sense, I attribute the truth of these men's words on manhood and culture to the natural law. See Romans 2 for its role in pagans doing what is required of them by the law.

5. The Disney film *Peter Pan* produced in 1953 was sourced in the original 1904 playwright of J. M. Berrie, *Peter Pan or The Boy Who Wouldn't Grow Up*.

6. Ashley Carman, "Spotify Reveals Joe Rogan's Podcast Numbers," Bloomberg.com, March 21, 2024, https://www.bloomberg.com/news/newsletters/2024-03-21/spotify-reveals-podcast-numbers-for-joe-rogan-alex-cooper-travis-kelce.

7. Dr. Jordan B. Peterson, "Maps of Meaning 06: Story & Metastory (Part 2)," YouTube, accessed February 21, 2025, https://www.youtube.com/watch?v=nsZ8XqHPjI4&t=7517s.

8. Ronald Rolheiser, *Sacred Fire: A Vision for a Deeper Human and Christian Maturity* (Image Books, 2014), 42–45. Within the work, Rolheiser also uses Nouwen to make this point. See Henri Nouwen, *The Genesee Diary* (Doubleday, 1976; reprint, Image Books, 1981).

9. George Janko, "The Jordan Peterson Interview," The George Janko Show, episode 58, YouTube, March 24, 2024, https://youtu.be/CyOteeLoTcM?si=ri-mdsfewtgv2lRC.

10. Jordan B. Peterson, "Message to the Christian Churches," YouTube, July 12, 2022, https://www.youtube.com/watch?v=e7ytLpO7mj0.

11. David Goggins, *Can't Hurt Me: Master Your Mind and Defy the Odds* (Lioncrest Publishing, 2018), 11–14.

12. Ryan Holiday, *The Daily Stoic: 366 Meditations on Wisdom, Perseverance, and the Art of Living* (Portfolio/Random House, 2016).

13. Augustine, *On Christian Teaching*, trans. R. P. H. Green (Oxford University Press, 1997), 47.

14. Augustine, *On Christian Teaching*, 47.

15. Herman Bavinck, *Reformed Ethics: Created, Fallen and Converted Humanity*, vol. 1 (Baker Academic, 2019), 156, 158.

16. Everett Piper, "'We Need Jesus,' Podcaster Rogan Says," *Washington Times*, March 3, 2024, https://www.washingtontimes.com/news/2024/mar/3/we-need-jesus-podcaster-rogan-says.

Chapter 3

1. Charles Spurgeon, "A Divided Heart," sermon, September 25, 1859, The Spurgeon Center, https://www.spurgeon.org/resource-library/sermons/a-divided-heart.

2. Grant R. Osborne, *Revelation: Baker Exegetical Commentary on the New Testament* (Baker Academic, 2002), 105.

3. *The Founder*, directed by John Lee Hancock, The Weinstein Company, January 20, 2017.

4. Osborne, *Revelation,* 208–9.

5. Osborne, *Revelation,* 205–6.

6. Jamin Goggin and Kyle Strobel, *The Way of the Dragon or the Way of the Lamb: Searching for Jesus' Path of Power in a Church that Has Abandoned It* (Thomas Nelson, 2017), 24.

7. Jeffrey M. Jones, "Church Attendance Has Declined in Most U.S. Religious Groups," Gallup, March 25, 2024, https://news.gallup.com/poll/642548/church-attendance-declined-religious-groups.aspx.

8. Dallas Willard, *Renovation of the Heart: Putting on the Character of Christ* (NavPress, 2002, 2012), 22–23.

9. N. T. Wright and Michael Bird, *Jesus and the Powers: Christian Political Witness in an Age of Totalitarian Terror and Dysfunctional Democracies* (Zondervan, 2024), 10–11, 17.

10. Jonathan Leeman, *Political Church: The Local Assembly as Embassy of Christ's Rule* (MI: InterVarsity Press, 2016), 82.

Chapter 4

1. As cited in conversation with John Ortberg, *Soul Keeping: Caring for the Most Important Part of You* (Zondervan, 2014), 23.

2. Though this isn't an academic work, I want to note that I endorse a Christocentric interpretation of the *imago Dei*. For further references, see Marc Cortez, *Resourcing Theological Anthropology: A Constructive Account of Humanity in the Light of Christ* (Zondervan, 2018), as well as Ryan S. Peterson's *The Imago Dei as Human Identity: A Theological Interpretation, Journal of Theological Interpretation Supplements*, vol. 14 (Eisenbrauns, 2016).

3. The image doesn't merely rest in ourselves as individual humans (whether that's our unique capacities or our relationships), but also as a God-bestowed ultimate end and *telos for humanity*, which is enabled by and grounded in Christ. Even in humanity's wretched state, God has not altered his calling for humanity or their identity—though the human person can be said to be disordered, broken, etc. See the references above, as well as John Kilner, *Dignity and Destiny: Humanity in the Image of God* (Eerdmans, 2015), 147–50 for a thorough account.

4. Richard Lints, *Identity and Idolatry: The Image of God and Its Inversion* (InterVarsity Press, 2015), 37.

5. J. Richard Middleton, *The Liberating Image: The Imago Dei in Genesis 1* (Brazos Press, 2005), 161.

6. Middleton, *The Liberating Image,* 161–64.

7. Middleton, *The Liberating Image*, 166.

8. John H. Walton, Victor H. Matthews, and Mark W. Chavalas, *The IVP Bible Background Commentary—Old Testament* (InterVarsity Press, 2000), 29.

9. Middleton, *The Liberating Image*, 176.

10. Middleton, *The Liberating Image*, 183.

11. See David Garland's discussion about Paul's assumption that one's sacrifice to an idol is naive, as it is truly to a demon, David E. Garland, *1 Corinthians: Baker Exegetical Commentary on the New Testament* (Baker Academic, 2003), 479–82.

12. Middleton, *The Liberating Image,* 108–10.

13. Middleton, *The Liberating Image,* 109.

14. Christopher J. H. Wright, *Old Testament Ethics for the People of God* (InterVarsity Press, 2004), 121.

15. For a few introductory works on the ancient Near East and the Old Testament, see John Walton, *The Lost World of Genesis 1* (InterVarsity Press, 2009).

16. Ryan S. Peterson, "Created and Constructed Identities," in *The Christian Doctrine of Humanity: Explorations in Constructive Dogmatics*, ed. Oliver Crisp and Fred Sanders (Zondervan, 2018), 138.

17. Middleton, *The Liberating Image*, 79–82.

18. Cornelius Plantinga Jr., *Not the Way It's Supposed to Be: A Breviary of Sin* (Eerdmans, 1995), 10.

19. J. Richard Middleton, *A New Heavens and a New Earth: Reclaiming Biblical Eschatology* (Baker Academic, 2014), 52–55.

20. N. T. Wright, *How God Became King: The Forgotten Story of the Gospels* (Harper Collins, 2012), 95.

21. Thomas F. Torrance, *Incarnation: The Person and Life of Christ* (InterVarsity Press, 2008), 114.

Chapter 5

1. Henri J. M. Nouwen, *The Return of the Prodigal Son: The Story of Homecoming* (Doubleday, 1992), 46–47.

2. Darrell L. Block, *Luke 9:51–24:53: Baker Exegetical Commentary on the New Testament* (Baker Academic, 1996), 1306, 1309.

3. Klyne R. Snodgrass, *Stories with Intent: A Comprehensive Guide to the Parables of Jesus* (Eerdmans, 2008), 141.

4. For those looking for further work on grasping the heart of the Father or prodigal son story, I highly recommend these two works, which were crucial for my own growth as a young man. See John Eldridge, *Fathered by God: Learning What Your Dad Could Never Teach You* (Thomas Nelson, 2009) and Timothy Keller, *The Prodigal God: Recovering the Heart of the Christian Faith* (Riverhead Books, 2008).

Chapter 6

1. Eugene Peterson, *The Jesus Way: A Conversation on the Ways that Jesus Is the Way* (Eerdmans, 2015), 22.

2. Stephen J. Nichols, *Bonhoeffer on the Christian Life: From the Cross, for the World* (Crossway, 2013), 22, 25. For a more in-depth biography, see Charles Marsh, *Strange Glory: A Life of Dietrich Bonhoeffer* (Vintage Books, 2015), 344–45.

3. Marsh, *Strange Glory*, 388–90.

4. Marsh, *Strange Glory*, 225.

5. Dietrich Bonhoeffer, *The Cost of Discipleship* (Touchstone Books/Simon & Schuster, [1937], 1995), 44–45.

6. Bonhoeffer, *The Cost of Discipleship*, 45.

7. Bonhoeffer, *The Cost of Discipleship*, 45.

8. Bonhoeffer, *The Cost of Discipleship*, 190–91.

9. J. I. Packer, *Keep in Step with The Spirit: Finding Fullness in Our Walk with God* (Baker Books, 1984, 2005), 51.

10. The phrase "every square inch" is a nod to Abraham Kuyper's famous expression on Christ's sovereignty and lordship. See Abraham Kuyper, "Sphere Sovereignty," in *Abraham Kuyper: A Centennial Reader*, ed. James D. Bratt (Eerdmans, 1998), 488.

11. Dallas Willard, *Knowing Christ Today: Why We Can't Trust Spiritual Knowledge* (HarperOne, 2009), 141.

12. Willard, *Knowing Christ Today*, 141.

13. A helpful reference point for this psalm is James M. Hamilton Jr., *Psalms: Volume 1:1–2*, Evangelical Biblical Theology Commentary (Lexham Academic, 2021), 249–63.

14. Timothy Ward, *Words of Life: Scripture as the Living and Active Word of God* (IVP Academic, 2009), 48.

15. Ward, *Words of Life*, 95.

16. Christopher A. Hall, "Reading Christ into the Heart: The Theological Foundations of Lectio Divina" in *Life in the Spirit: Spiritual Formation in Theological Perspective*, ed. Jeffrey P. Greenman and George Kalantzis (IVP Academic, 2009), 143.

17. Hall, "Reading Christ into the Heart," 144–45.

18. Richard Foster, *The Celebration of Discipline: The Path to Spiritual Growth* (Harper Collins, 1978, 1988, 1998), 84–85.

Chapter 7

1. John Calvin, *Institutes of the Christian Religion, Vol. 1*, ed. John T. McNeill, trans. Ford Lewis Battles (Westminster John Knox: Modern Library, 1960), 108.

2. Eugene H. Peterson, *A Long Obedience in the Same Direction: Discipleship in an Instant Society* (IVP, 1980, 2000), 11–12.

3. Peterson, *A Long Obedience in the Same Direction*, 11.

4. Peterson, *A Long Obedience in the Same Direction*, 11–12.

5. This notion of adopting and projecting misrepresentations of God stems from the work of Peter Enns, *The NIV Application Commentary: Exodus* (Zondervan, 2000), 569.

6. G. K. Beale, *We Become What We Worship: A Biblical Theology of Idolatry* (IVP, 2008), 305.

7. Nancy Pearcey, *The Toxic War on Masculinity: How Christianity Reconciles the Sexes* (Baker Books, 2023), 101.

8. Pearcey, *The Toxic War on Masculinity*, 72, 75–76.

9. Pearcey, *The Toxic War on Masculinity*, 76.

Chapter 8

1. John Ortberg, *The Me I Want to Be: Becoming God's Best Version of You* (Zondervan, 2014), 24–25.

2. Quinn Dworkowski, Family Law Attorneys, "Orange County Divorce Rate 2025, https://www.orangecountyfamilylaw.com/blog/orange-county-divorce-rate/.

3. John Mark Comer, *The Ruthless Elimination of Hurry* (WaterBrook, 2019), 19.

4. Comer, *The Ruthless Elimination of Hurry*, 19–20.

5. Peter Scazzero, *Emotionally Healthy Discipleship* (Zondervan Reflective, 2021), 50.

Chapter 9

1. Tim Keller, Twitter, April 30, 2014, x.com/timkellernyc/status/461525634758742016.

2. Joseph Loconte, *A Hobbit, a Wardrobe and a Great War: How J. R. R. Tolkien and C. S. Lewis Rediscovered Faith, Friendship,*

and Heroism in the Cataclysm of 1914–1918 (Nelson Books, 2015), 20–21.

3. Loconte, *A Hobbit, a Wardrobe, and a Great War*, 91.

4. Loconte, *A Hobbit, a Wardrobe, and a Great War*, xiii–xiv.

5. Loconte, *A Hobbit, a Wardrobe, and a Great War*, 129–30.

6. Loconte, *A Hobbit, a Wardrobe, and a Great War*, 132.

7. Loconte, *A Hobbit, a Wardrobe, and a Great War*, 130.

8. Loconte, *A Hobbit, a Wardrobe, and a Great War*, 133.

9. Loconte, *A Hobbit, a Wardrobe, and a Great War*, 133, citing Walter Hooper, ed., *The Collected Letters of C. S. Lewis*, vol.1 (HarperSanFrancisco, 2004), 974.

10. Loconte, *A Hobbit, a Wardrobe, and a Great War*, 179, citing Hooper, ed., *The Collected Letters of C. S. Lewis*, vol. 2, 501.

11. C. S. Lewis, *The Four Loves* (HarperOne, 1960), 114.

12. Bradley J. Birzer, *J. R. R. Tolkien's Sanctifying Myth: Understanding Middle-earth* (ISI Books, 2003), 41.

13. J. R. R. Tolkien, *The Return of the King: Being the Third Part of The Lord of the Rings* (Houghton Mifflin, 1994), 919.

14. Birzer, *J. R. R. Tolkien's Sanctifying Myth*, 105.

15. Birzer, *J. R. R. Tolkien's Sanctifying Myth*, 105–6.

Chapter 10

1. Dietrich Bonhoeffer, *The Cost of Discipleship* (Touchstone Books/Simon & Schuster, [1937], 1995), 91.

2. D. A. Carson, *Matthew: Chapters 1–12,* The Expositors Bible Commentary with the New International Version (Zondervan, 1995), 194. Also see R. T. France, *The Gospel of Matthew*, New International Commentary on the New Testament, (Eerdmans, 2007), 296.

3. In Matthew 5:1–2, notice Jesus desiring to be away from the masses with just his disciples. A crowd clearly followed him amid this effort to be more private.

4. Dan B. Allender and Tremper Longman III, *The Cry of the Soul: How Our Emotions Reveal Our Deepest Questions About God* (NavPress, 2015), 7.

5. Allender and Longman III, *The Cry of the Soul,* 2.

6. Chip Dodd, *The Voice of the Heart* (Sage Hill, 2014), 157.

7. Allender and Longman III, *The Cry of the Soul,* 25.

8. Dodd, *The Voice of the Heart*, 38.

Chapter 11

1. Francis Schaeffer, *Death in the City, vol. 4, Complete Works of Francis A. Schaeffer: A Christian Worldview, A Christian View of the Church* (Crossway, 1982), 230.

2. Carl R. Trueman, *The Rise and Triumph of the Modern Self: Cultural Amnesia, Expressive Individualism, and the Road to the Sexual Revolution* (Crossway, 2020), 96. Trueman borrows the term and framing of deathworks from Philip Rieff, *My Life Among the Deathworks: Illustrations of the Aesthetics as Authority (Sacred Order/Social Order)* vol. 1, ed. Kenneth S. Piver (University of Virginia Press, 2006), 7, 98–99.

3. Trueman, *The Rise and Triumph of the Modern Self,* 97.

4. Trueman, *The Rise and Triumph of the Modern Self,* 99.

5. Trueman, *The Rise and Triumph of the Modern Self,* 98–99.

6. Augustine, *The City of God Against the Pagans*, ed. R. W. Dyson (Cambridge University Press, 1998), 609. For Augustine, the concept of self-love is not inherently sinful but takes proper form when aligned with the love of God. See Oliver O'Donovan,

The Problem of Self-Love in St. Augustine (Wipf and Stock Publishers, 1980), 147.

7. It's common to understand Matthew 10:1–15 as specific to the apostles, while the remainder of the chapter is broader in nature due to Jesus's eschatological tone. See R. T. France, *The Gospel of Matthew,* New International Commentary on the New Testament (Eerdmans, 2007), 389.

8. Dallas Willard, *Renovation of the Heart: Putting on the Character of Christ* (NavPress, 2002, 2012), 64.

Appendix 1

1. These steps can also be retraced in a more academic conversation in Christopher A. Hall, "Reading Christ into the Heart: The Theological Foundations of Lectio Divina" in *Life in the Spirit: Spiritual Formation in Theological Perspective,* ed. Jeffrey P. Greenman and George Kalantzis (IVP Academic, 2009), 146, 158.

Appendix 2

1. Adele Ahlberg Calhoun, *Spiritual Disciplines Handbook: Practices That Transform Us* (InterVarsity Press, 2005), 92–94.